Almost a Great Escape

Also by Tyler Trafford
The Métis Girl
Alexander's Way
The Story of Blue Eye

ALMOST THE GREAT ESCAPE

A Found Story

TYLER TRAFFORD

GOOSE LANE

Edited by John Sweet.
Cover and page design by Chris Tompkins.
All photos courtesy of the author unless otherwise stated.
Cover image of Alice Tyler courtesy of the McCord Museum.
Printed in Canada.
10 9 8 7 6 5 4 3 2 1

Library and Archives Canada Cataloguing in Publication

Trafford, Tyler, 1949-
Almost a great escape: a found story / Tyler Trafford.

Also issued in electronic format.
ISBN 978-0-86492-686-9

1. Trafford, Alice — Correspondence. 2. Müller, Jens — Correspondence.
3. Trafford, Tyler, 1949- — Family. 4. Stalag Luft III. 5. Prisoner-of-war escapes — Poland — Żaga´n. 6. World War, 1939-1945 — Prisoners and prisons, German.
7. Mothers and sons. 8. Authors, Canadian (English) — 20th century — Biography. I. Title.

PS8589.R335Z53 2013   C813'.54   C2012-906316-9

Goose Lane Editions acknowledges the generous support of the Canada Council for the Arts, the Government of Canada through the Canada Book Fund (CBF), and the Government of New Brunswick through the Department of Tourism, Heritage, and Culture.

Goose Lane Editions
500 Beaverbrook Court, Suite 330
Fredericton, New Brunswick
CANADA E3B 5X4
www.gooselane.com

For Judy, Sharnee, and Nicolas

"Please Alice remember that I'll come back…"
Jens Müller

11   The Campbell's Beef Noodle Soup Box

23   The Jens Album

145   63 Days

165   Terms of an Engagement

175   Consequences

229   Destinations

247   My Search for Jens Müller

267   Acknowledgements

THE CAMPBELL'S
BEEF NOODLE SOUP BOX

ONE GOOD THING

My mother's name was Alice Tyler. The story of her One Good Thing begins at her funeral in April 2004 and ends 60 years earlier, in March 1944, when 76 World War II airmen break out of Stalag Luft III, the Nazi prison camp in Sagan, Poland. The Great Escape made into a Steve McQueen film: 73 recaptured, 50 executed. Only 3 made it home.

In 1961, when I was 12, Alice knew something was going to happen to us that I wouldn't understand. Instead of trying to explain it, she gave me one of her favourite books: *The Old Man and the Sea* by Ernest Hemingway. I still have the book. It is a first edition, printed in 1952. It could be valuable today to collectors because Hemingway won a Pulitzer Prize with it—except our dog chewed a corner. It's a small book, only 140 pages. I still read it whenever I feel small in a big world. I have read it hundreds of times.

The plot is simple. An old Cuban fisherman named Santiago fishes alone, far out on the Gulf Stream where nobody else dares to go. There he hooks the biggest marlin he has ever seen: 18 feet long.

For two days and nights the fish tows Santiago's small skiff toward the floating horizon. The line rips through the calluses of Santiago's already scarred hands. His admiration for the fish's courage and endurance becomes love. The fish is the most noble experience of his life.

Waiting for his return is Manolin, the boy the old man has been teaching to fish.

On the third day, Santiago is able to pull the marlin close. He drives his harpoon into its heart. He still loves it after it is dead. Blood swirls into the current. The marlin is too long to load onto his skiff, so he ties it to the side. Then sharks attack. Santiago uses the last of his strength defending the marlin.

He sails through the night and into the harbour. All the sharks have left him is a skeleton.

In the morning Manolin finds Santiago asleep in his shack. He sees his teacher's ripped hands and begins to cry. On his way to buy coffee for the old man he sees the remains of the marlin in the harbour. He begins to cry again.

Alice told me I must be like Santiago and catch a truly big fish — The One Good Thing in my life. Never give up. Nothing else matters. Not even the sharks that come afterwards.

She liked that expression, One Good Thing. We all have one, she would say. When life shows up with a package and your name is on it. Take it. Don't hesitate. The opportunity will never come again.

She told me this in so many ways that I knew it had a significance to her wrapped around something she kept hidden.

I often wanted to ask her what the One Good Thing in her life had been. But how can a boy ask his mother what it is she won't talk about?

After I read the book again, I asked her what would have happened to Santiago if his fish had gotten away.

She kissed me on the forehead. "A fisherman like Santiago keeps his truly big fish in his heart, whether he brings it to the shore or not. What or who we love never gets away. We fight the sharks forever to remember that love. Maybe one day you'll write a book with that ending."

I was Manolin. My mother was Santiago. For twelve years she had been teaching me to be just like her.

Then I was alone.

MY GOODBYE MOTHER

Alice gave me her name, Tyler. My older brother got my father's name, Ted (Teddy).

Alice taught me everything she considered important. She taught me how to care, how to laugh, and how to live my own life.

She taught me to read from *New Yorkers* and novels. She taught me to ride a horse, swim, ski, and ignore people who said a boy couldn't decide for himself.

Because we were more like friends than mother/son, it wasn't hard for me to see she kept something hidden that she would never talk about. Maybe she thought I would eventually figure it out for myself. Figuring things out for myself was an important part of being with Alice.

People often said Alice was blue eyed blonde slim beautiful. I always said she was strong. She had the strongest soft hands of any person I would ever know. You couldn't break her grip. She always held me safe.

When I was six, I came home from my first day of school and told her I didn't think I would learn anything there. She didn't argue. A month later she introduced me to Mrs. Bilton, a grade three teacher who was willing to try me in her class. Mrs. Bilton divided her class into animal groups and pasted bluebirds, squirrels, and robins on their scribblers. She rewarded students with gold stars and pinned the best pages on the walls. I tore the bluebird off my scribbler and pulled my gold stars from the wall. The last time Alice ever came to my school was to persuade Mrs. Bilton that I would do fine as a group of one. She wanted me to be able to figure things out for myself. Mrs. Bilton said I was already doing that and I didn't have to be a bluebird.

If the snow was good, Alice took me out of school to go skiing. If the grass was green, we went riding. We considered report cards unimportant.

Alice protected me from my father. And paid for it. He was a charming, loveless aristocrat—and a good liar—who liked to reach over and rap my knuckles with a soup spoon whenever I spilled food or wasn't sitting up straight. He said he was teaching me British manners. I had to take the rap then, or the belt later. He expected gold stars from a lad of my possibilities. Alice changed the subject when she could.

My father was not my mother's One Good Thing. I couldn't imagine he had one, and I wished my mother would tell me what hers was.

Maybe she had missed her One Good Thing. Maybe she had waited too long. Maybe she had made a mistake. If that were true, I had figured out who the mistake was.

I may have been only a lad—as my father used to call me in his British way—but I was old enough to see he didn't like how close Alice and I were, the way we laughed at the same jokes, and how we disappeared into the mountains leaving him at home with the children and the nanny. He worked late those days. I was too young to know what that really meant.

But I wasn't too young to figure out he didn't like my ignore you attitude when told what to do by him or by anybody else. I knew he didn't like this and many other things about me. I didn't know why it mattered to him what I did. As far as I could tell, what I did was none of his or anybody else's business.

When I was 13, my mother of summer horses and rivers didn't want me to see the slow dying coming for her: alcoholism, breast cancer, polymyalgia, and an unfaithful, bullying husband.

The day I was sent away to boarding school, she stood beside me on the railway platform in Calgary. It was a tearless farewell.

I would never live at home again for more than a few months at a time. My five brothers and one sister would soon be strangers to me.

I would never see the mother again who didn't wave from the railway platform. I would remember her as My Goodbye Mother: the mother I once had.

When the train brought me home for Christmas, Alice's silent blue eyes told me there was no going back for us. As much as I didn't want to, I would have to face life on my own. I would have to figure things out for myself, the way My Goodbye Mother had taught me. She had faith in me.

She had 41 years of dying ahead. She expected I would find better things to do with my life than wait around for that.

I took all the memories a boy's heart could carry and buried them in silence. No words, no flowers, no crying. Just a flat grey stone rolled onto my forgetting place. I would always love My Goodbye Mother, but it got harder and harder to remember her. Finally I couldn't remember I had a forgetting place.

The Alice who replaced My Goodbye Mother lived drunk fighting and drugged in the upstairs bedroom. Radiation burned lungs connected by clear tubes to an oxygen machine. Pills, magazines, and books spilling from her bed and recliner onto the floor. My father slept in his study. I visited whenever I thought he would be out.

Some days I would sit by her bed while she slept and wonder how this had happened. When I left, I would kiss her forehead. I expected she would know I had been there. On days when I visited Alice and she was awake, she'd pour a toothbrush glass of Smirnoff from a hidden bottle and light up a du Maurier. She enjoyed a cigarette with her oxygen, the mechanical bellows pulsing spurts of life support into her nostrils. Smoking was her shrugged shoulder acknowledgment of death, not its denial. Santiago knew the sharks would come. He didn't argue the inevitable, but he made them pay for every bite of the marlin's flesh.

When she was drinking hard, Alice would hit any sharks nearby with embarrassing truths, or what she decided were truths. But in all her Smirnoff fights with my father, her children, and her few friends, she never used her own One Good Thing as a weapon. I never heard her step into a fight with "If only I had…" She was always a no going back person.

Before she went to the hospital for the last time, she called me into her bedroom. "I'm leaving you something special," she said.

"Thank you," I said. I didn't have any expectations. I didn't ask any questions because I knew all she had left were/was good intentions.

She named me the executor of her estate. Anything left after her funeral expenses would go to my father.

Her six other children voted to host an extravagant send off. They didn't know about a 13-year-old boy's railway station goodbye. They wanted a McInnis and Holloway departure; prayers, hymns, and a glowing eulogy at Christ Church in Elbow Park; an all you can drink public reception at the Calgary Golf and Country Club with cascades of flowers, hot and cold hors d'oeuvres, and a private supper. First class exclusive and expensive. What I didn't know then was that this funeral would be a repeat of a Westmount, Montreal, funeral: one she hadn't attended. I didn't know much about Alice's Before Me life.

I didn't argue the family's big spending vote. I believed My Goodbye Mother would have enjoyed the irony of a farewell Country Club bender for an alcoholic wife and mother. She appreciated irony.

My father kept track of the funeral expenses, insisting anything over the cost of a basic cremation, church service, and burial of ashes be covered by her children, not by her estate. He was surprised but pleased to learn she had prepaid their Eden Brook Memorial Gardens burial plots. The savings meant I would be writing him a bigger cheque.

I didn't have a chance to think much about ashes to ashes until the half dark Christ Church funeral service began. I sat anonymously in a middle pew as my Anglican father and siblings paraded in from the vestry. They were a grieving family of front row strangers. I was a passerby. I had rolled a grey stone over my grieving. Alone. Long ago. Silent and tearless now.

In front of me, the altar. The deceased's photograph on an oak table in the aisle. Behind me, the baptistery. The congregation a pause between birth and death.

A boy wearing a red flannel shirt patterned with gold horseshoes and silver lariats walks beside the pews, searching each one, then moving on. He stops and slides across the polished oak to my side. "I remember her," he says, his back to the altar.

He has happy hazel eyes and is unconcerned that he might be disturbing the service.

He says: "I remember she woke me in the almost light, tugging the blankets from my shoulder. 'We're going riding,' she whispered to me. 'Let the others sleep. Get dressed and come to the corral. I'll start saddling the horses.'"

This imperturbable boy seems a memory found to me.

"I was seven years old and used to disappearing with her," he says. "She took me places where nobody else went. I liked her crazy strong go anywhere do anything daring. I liked her a lot.

"We followed the Bow River west. When we stopped to rest the horses, she gave me a tinfoil wrapped breakfast of thick sliced toast with bacon and jam. The grass was wet with dew.

"'It's a fuck of a life,' she told me. 'It's a fuck of a life if you don't live it your own way.'

"I wasn't old enough to answer, but I understood what she meant. I wished I had the words to tell her before it was too late.

"At noon," the boy continued, "we hobbled the horses in the sun flickering through silent spruce trees. She held my horse's reins and drank vodka from a silver flask. I could feel her blue eyes watching me as I pulled apart a handful of bacon. She never ate when we went riding.

"'I'm going to do something for you,' she said, pulling a spruce branch through her hands. 'Unbutton your shirt.' She rubbed the broken needles bleeding sap over my chest and back. 'Remember the smell of alone. Remember who you are today.'

"'Never forget what I am showing you,' she said, sprinkling baptismal drops of vodka burn onto my lips and tongue.

"Then she gave me the reins to my horse. 'Close your hands. Tight. Never let go of your horse. Never let go of who you are.'"

The boy in the red flannel shirt pauses, then says, "One day you'll remember the sun standing still. The horses grazing. You'll remember the slur of the river. The silent shifting trees. The gentle touch of her hands."

He slides across the pew to the aisle and walks out of the church.

The mourners picked up their folded funeral notes with photos of the deceased. I stood with them to sing the hymns. I knelt to pray. The ritual of compliance. Never easy for me.

In my wandering thoughts, I am beside Alice's bed. She wants something to look forward to, and I don't mind being an accomplice to that forlorn expectation. Life after death. What did it matter?

Some people, I tell her, believe you will be reunited with everybody you love after you pass over the ocean of death. I thought this vision had a satisfyingly vague ecumenical cloudiness. She smiled and took a deep drag on her cigarette.

"Maybe my father will be there. Maybe other people I loved will be there."

Who? I should have asked but didn't. Those impassable blue eyes of hers could always stop a none of my business question before I dared to ask. I'm glad now I didn't ask. What tragedy her too soon for me explanation would have been.

There are many things it is better to find out on your own.

During the reverend's never speak ill of the dead eulogy, I heard muffled giggles from the office dressed women gossiping in the back pews. They knew the dirt on the family. Her drinking. His women. A man needs comfort when his wife turns to drink.

I am cold on the church steps to kissing cheeks.

Yes, she was brave fighting the cancer. Yes, her nicotine poisoned, radiation burned lungs barely kept her alive.

And the polymyalgia?

Yes, nobody deserves to suffer like that.

How's your father holding up?

We ignore infidelity after funerals. Fine.

It was easy. I didn't feel a thing.

Then the surprise whisper in my ear. "You are so much like her." My mother's friend. "G." She turns down the steps while I wonder why.

I expect some Country Club hand shakers would have been surprised to hear my inheritance was a Campbell's Beef Noodle Soup Box of old letters and creased photos. The top criss-crossed closed. Sealed with tape. To be opened later. It didn't look special to me. But, if you love an alcoholic, you can't expect her to remember or live up to her promises, so this cardboard bequest couldn't be a disappointment.

The box reminded me of My Goodbye Mother's many promises to get organized. I have to get back on track, she would say with good intentions as she tried lists, notes, diaries, filing cabinets, and manila envelopes. Systems didn't work for her. When were you on track? I would ask, and she'd laugh and kiss me. You know, she said.

She dashed off messages to herself spontaneously writing on whatever paper was handiest. At a new home show she saw an open desk with paper and envelopes laid out as if the owner were about to write a letter. She wrote one to My Dearest Alice and people wandering through the home always stopped to read it.

Her chequebook was written in paragraphs with words she'd discovered. *Dishabille*—a lost Jane Austen word. Late 1700s. Dressed in a deliberately careless or casual manner. What did we like about Jane's books? So polite. So restrained. Unrealistic, she said and we kept reading.

I didn't attend the irrelevant family burial of her ashes at Eden Brook. But I was drawn to her grave when the sun turned the mountains close and clear. Stopping by now and then to say hello. Not expecting a reply.

In September, a time of dread for me who lives brightest in summers of flowing fast rivers, horses, and the smell of spruce, I opened the soup box.

A disorganization of time and places. A photo of me in a silver and leather frame age six on a pinto pony. A wallet sized photo of Tyler and Alice blonde thin and smiling. Another of me on a horse.

Bundles of You're So Beautiful letters rolled tight with elastic bands. I peel off a letter: 1940. Before Me. The war years 1939-1945. Young swains writing Alice Tyler. Quite a few from Don tied with a frayed blue ribbon. Very chatty. He's sure of something. Who is he? Is it the war that makes these young men write you age 16 or 17 with hope. Imagine keeping these letters for 60 years. Maybe it was reassuring to know those days had once been yours.

And then I found the Jens Album. On the bottom of the box. Love dressed in dishabille.

THE JENS ALBUM

THE RESURRECTION

At first I thought the crumbling, hand tied album had been inheritance included by mistake. It couldn't have belonged to Alice. She wouldn't have had the patience to meticulously organize its hundreds of letters, telegrams, and photographs.

But the letters were addressed to *My Dearest Alice* and signed *Your Jens*. Second Lieutenant Jens Müller. Royal Norwegian Air Force. His 1941 fighter pilot letters of love begin while he is stationed at Little Norway, a training field outside Toronto for the young Norwegians who had escaped the Nazi occupation. Recruits without a homeland. Preparing to be shipped overseas. Then letters from England. Hurricanes and Spitfires. Flying combat missions over the British Channel. Precise thinking. Precise handwriting.

Photos. Alice and Jens skiing. Jens's portrait in uniform signed *With All My Love*. Tall. Fair-haired. Slender. A skier. A motorcyclist. A pilot. His Hurricane fighter aircraft named *Odin*. The heroic Norseman. She is his Dearest Alice. When the war is over, he will return for her. She can be sure of it.

I believe him.

I read letters at random about Before Me Jens. He has just returned to his training camp. He's been skiing at the Tyler family's resort, the Alpine Inn, in St. Marguerite's, north of Montreal. He has crashed in flight training. Unauthorized. Under power lines. He sends this photo. His plane nosedived into the trees. Reprimanded. He spends his nights in an air force jail and his days flying. He doesn't mind. He has time to think. The other pilots have

"With all my love." Alice kept this portrait of Jens hidden with her album.

nicknamed him Poker Face. He is cautious about the future. No commitment except his love for you. Distant cool.

He writes I cannot promise you anything Alice except I will always love you and I will come back for you after the war. I am a fighter pilot. I have no education. I will wear your pin inside my flying helmet. I will not hold you to your promise.

I can see Alice alone in her bedroom, oxygen tubes coiled beneath her recliner. A Smirnoff bottle under her *New Yorker*s. The album across her lap. She remembers love.

At least she has kept that. It is hers. Forever.

My Dearest Alice received 99 letters, cards, and telegrams from Your Jens. I assume she wrote as many, as he often thanked her for sending two and three letters a day.

The letters were written to an Alice Tyler aspiring to be a writer. An Alice unable to tell her parents she was engaged to a Norwegian fighter pilot flying Spitfires over the British Channel. An Alice Tyler who would be My Goodbye Mother.

Until I read the Jens Album, I had never known my grandmother's name. That was how seldom Alice had talked to me about her parents, her brother and her sisters, about her life before she married Ted, my father. It was as if she had taken the first 20 years of her life and stuffed them into a Campbell's soup box for me to separate from her ashes.

Now her Alice Tyler years are on my desk. Elastic wrapped rolls of letters. Bundles of clippings, photos, and telegrams. The Jens Album. I have found her Before Me.

I am hesitating and almost criss-cross close this box of good intentions when My Goodbye Mother reminds me that, if I want an answer that is my own, I have to figure it out for myself.

I leave the Jens Album open on my desk.

I am so much like her.

MANOLIN

There is more in this soup box than an album love story; although I am fascinated by my wanting to know the why of that story's ending. The box has become unique—of special significance—in my thoughts. It has a title—The Campbell's Soup Box—just as the album is now The Jens Album.

What else of My Goodbye Mother is hidden?

Much more, I suspect. Too much for The Campbell's Soup Box to hold.

I will need a suitcase. I choose one of hers. Navy blue with brass zippers. "I'm staying put now," she had said, bequeathing it to me before Eden Brook, full of magazines and empties from beneath her recliner.

My list of mnemonics increases: My Goodbye Mother, The Jens Album, The One Good Thing, The Campbell's Soup Box, and now Alice's Suitcase. I begin filling the suitcase with messages from My Goodbye Mother's no going back life: postcards, Christmas cards, lists of unusual words, letters, portraits of rarely mentioned parents and grandparents, *The Old Man and the Sea*.

I am again the boy in pyjamas reading with her Jane Austen's marry well novels. Henry Miller's *Tropic of Cancer*. John Steinbeck's *Cannery Row*. She wanted life with the skin peeled away, and these writers peeled it back with language she understood. Baptism language.

I remember her reminding me, "It's a fuck of a life if you don't live it your own way."

I had forgotten but remember the horse she gave me. I might have been eight. She tells me I will have to learn to ride that horse on my own. If I do, I will always be able to go anywhere. Do anything.

Too late now to thank her for this metaphor.

I had forgotten but remember now lying across a deep stuffed armchair, my feet hanging over the side. I am ten or eleven. I'm holding a book open while I am thinking about my mother. I think she has a secret.

She is leaning back in the deep stuffed couch beside me. She has her feet up on a low wooden table and a glass of vodka in her hand.

We are alone in the house and it is quiet.

She is looking into her glass as if it holds her secret.

"This isn't the time to be thinking," she says, keeping her blue eyes to herself. "This is the time for knowing."

"Knowing what?" I ask, wondering if she will tell me her secret.

She turns toward me. "To want nothing and to expect nothing. To live a good for nothing life."

I am used to her talking to me in a way nobody else does.

She revolves the glass slowly in her hand and takes a drink. "It is tempting to be important and want everything."

She is holding me gently in her blue eyes. "Try not to forget your good for nothing mother."

Suddenly I feel like crying and in my holding back I guess her secret. She is going to leave me. I will be alone.

She takes another long drink of vodka and then it is quiet again.

I begin talking to her in the quiet at Eden Brook. I open Alice's Suitcase on yesterday's machine grazed grass and show her what I have found. I read aloud My Goodbye Mother memories I began writing after I opened The Campbell's Soup Box and found The Jens Album: The Horse Dance, Before the Forgetting Came. I will write more, I tell her. When I have more words.

Call me Alice, she reminds me here when I call her Mum. You're not a boy. Write the way you think. Let me hear your voice mixed up in tenses of second and third persons. At Eden Brook we don't expect report card grammar.

I tell Alice we have a suitcase of messages to discuss: Jens, the Alpine Inn, Westmount, the Flanagans, Venezuela, the Tylers, Canmore, and a lot of fragments that I still don't know where they belong, such as why you forgot so many days but never my wife Judy's birthday, March 24, and the day Pierre Trudeau said Hello Alice as you stepped into the elevator of a Calgary hotel.

I understand the you and I of those moments, she answers. You will find the impossibleness of my forgetting March 24. You will find Pierre's crossing place.

Finding begins with remembering. Talking. Reading. Together we loved Santiago who despite his 84 days of bad luck rowed into the unknown and caught a marlin so alive and so powerful that the old fisherman has to slow the line screaming through his hands each time the fish surges. Admirable, you said. It's a giving up life if you let go. We loved his fish.

In my flannel pyjamas I chose to read aloud for us the final scene where a tourist sees the marlin's 18 feet of skeleton drifting in the harbour but has no idea what Santiago has caught. Is it a shark? How would a tourist know the alone triumph of Santiago raising the patched sail of his skiff to guide the flesh ripped high finned marlin onto the night shore?

Your blonde hair drifting across my pillow. You read an earlier scene. It is the still dark morning of Santiago's third day at sea. The marlin surfaces and from the splash Santiago knows how big the fish is and knows he must show the fish he loves how much pain he is willing to endure.

And all I had ever caught were Bow River cold Dolly Varden. Big to me fish dancing silver twisting high above the rapids.

Not many years later, I pull the blankets over your cancer fatigued shoulders. We lean against each other on the couch like mother and son sharing again *The Old Man and the Sea.*

While you sleep I remember for us the first pages. Manolin wonders whether Santiago, his teacher, should sail alone onto the Gulf Stream. What if you catch a too big fish?

Santiago replies with quiet confidence. He is still strong and has a lifetime of tricks to rely upon.

In the last pages, Manolin sees how much he still has to learn about fishing. About life.

I know you will wake on this couch with pain. It is an always with you shark, tearing away your possibilities. I have learned now too late how much you could endure. More than Santiago I believe. You sleep sailing Your Jens Album to a shore I cannot see.

How could a tourist of life know the value of this remnant won from the deep of your being?

For an hour you wash like repeating waves against my skiff. I am quiet.

Fishing on a rhythmic sea. My hook drifts in fathoms of darkness where a marvellous something swims. A silent never come again possibility. My One Good Thing.

So now I write and cry our saltwater yesterdays. For us I will remember everything before the forgetting came.

"FOR KEEPS"

At Eden Brook, I am reading graveside letters aloud from your Jens Album. I particularly like reading this to the point letter written by Jens four months after you met at your family's ski resort. I find him honourable in his two promises: he will always love you and he will return for you after the war.

I worry about you loving a fighter pilot with rare chances of living long enough to keep his promises.

I find honest his reminder that, as a pilot without an education or money, he can only do his best to "make good" when the war is over. He knows that, in your debutante Montreal, education and money count for more than a Norwegian pilot's promises.

April 6, 1941

Dearest!

Back again after a nice trip to Montreal. I miss you so very much Alice. I never even dreamt I could love anyone so much as I love you. Perhaps you don't think I act as if I do when we are together. But I assure you darling, I would do anything for you, and to be able to be with you. I wish I could find the words to thank you for the lovely time we spent together. I shall never forget it as long as I live. Please Alice remember that I'll come back to you some day in the not so very distant future, and that will be "for keeps," please remember that when the "competitors" turn up too. My only thought from now will be to find some way to be able to make good after the war is over, and I will.

Although you don't like it I'll close now. I wish I could hug you Alice. I'll have to imagine I do.

Remember I love you Alice, with all my heart.

Jens

EDEN BROOK

October. It is your birthday this month. I happen to be driving by. It has been six months since the Christ Church funeral. I sit with the suitcase where you said you would like to watch the sun brushed mountains.

On the grass I do not ask why, after 60 years of waiting for the impossible to change, you still chose ashes to ashes husband and wife side by side forever. What about Your Jens? I do not ask.

Your gravestone questions me. Shouldn't it read Alice Patricia?

I walk to the graveyard office, where they don't ask about the suitcase. They explain politely that the gravestone is a Memorial, and I am asking about the Memorial Inscription. Thank you. Tell me more. They are very nice and after a little discussion they photocopy the form you signed. There it is, your signature. This is what you wanted. Not your given names. Alice Patricia. You chose your maiden name. Alice Tyler. To be remembered that way. My name too. Tyler. We are linked inexorably. Wrong, you say. Inextricably.

After I add the Memorial mnemonic to my list, I thank you for leaving me a simple estate to take care of. Before you checked into the hospital you lined up the artifacts of your children's lives on the dining-room table as if we would all choose the same day to run away from home. Go. Have a nice life. Remember when I packed my important stuff and ran away. You made me a jam sandwich in case I got hungry and let me go down 38th Avenue in my blue jeans and red shirt with gold horseshoes and silver lariats never to return. No more Christopher Robin school for me. Then you happened to

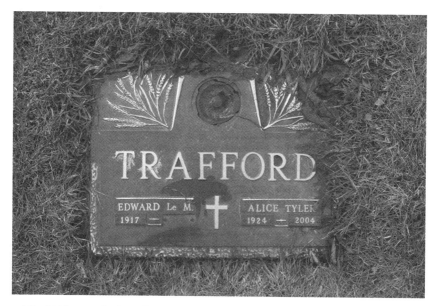

Alice's Memorial, Canada. Here, at Eden Brook Memorial Gardens overlooking the Rocky Mountains, Tyler brought a suitcase of keepsakes to show Alice. Later, he began reading his Goodbye Mother stories to her.

be driving by in the wood panelled station wagon. What confidence I had in you. You let me figure things out for myself.

It would have been a nice touch if you had packed a jam sandwich in my Campbell's Soup Box of memories before you died. Except it was you who was doing the leaving.

Dad manipulated. He wanted to keep our childhoods on the table awhile longer. Afraid without that hold we would desert him. It looked unseemly for us, he said, to be looting the house the day after the funeral. Ted Jr. called him churlish. Good word and Dad relented. The candlesticks and spoons clinked and clunked out to the cars. Me walking wondering if you might happen to be driving by.

I sit on billowing grass inside a Bow River meadow. Lost without you. Wondering if you will just happen to ride by. Will you hold me in your blue eyed nothingness? Open the silence. Help me understand my loving you.

THE HORSE DANCE

They are waiting for us. Corrals of hot dust horses stamping morning flies. From McBride's, the outfitters on the east side of Old Canmore. Belle chewing oats in a feed bag. Geoff crawls under her and there she stands front leg in the air waiting for him to move on. Your nobody get excited look as you pick him up.

Pack horses, trail horses. They come and go. A week, a day. Next time can we get Belle? I listen to you asking tobacco chewing Mrs. McBride her silver belt buckle shining in my eyes.

And horse sale horses. The Calgary auction: $40...$60! Some too wild to ride and then they are gone. Replaced. You ride them and then I can try.

Twinkle. The first beautiful horse and $65 at the auction. Untried and elegant. No wonder you bought her. Black with a white star hidden under her forelock. Fine legs, small feet. Maybe Teddy could ride her one day. I still ride plough horses. Old horses. Tired horses. Always eating grass horses. Twinkle never stopped. You circled and circled her on the golf course. Sweating. And she sidepasses along the trails, ready to run, wanting to run, and at night she is over the corral fence. And I watch you from the yard rail. You ride straight as a young man. Your destiny as right as your smile of excitement. You and Twinkle shine. The moment of mystery. It is the horse dance in wet heat.

When I was alone, I saddled her. Not scared at all. Just wanting to know if I could. Alone. The boys...you are taking them to visit friends. I'm small and climb on from the fence and suddenly she ran. Straight and I've never felt so much fast. I pull until she turns to the left. And then we circle cantering to a trot and I'm wondering how I'm getting off. She won't walk. She won't stop.

Maybe I'll drop inside the circle when she slows. I kick the stirrup from my right foot and swing up my heel. And her back feet go sliding under her and she is stopped. I put my foot back in the stirrup and we're trotting. I try it again, lifting my foot and her back feet slide under her and she is stopped.

I understand. She's a cowboy's roping horse. My foot coming out of the stirrup is a sliding stop signal after the calf is roped. I play with her like that for a while. I start to ride her with one hand. She neck reins and not just a little. She can spin and be gone the other way at a loose touch.

Then you are driving up in the station wagon. I see your don't get excited walk as you tell me to stop. Back feet sliding under her and you don't reach for the rein. I do it alone. That's a knowing we have. I do it alone.

The truck came into our nothingness a few days later, and you and I stand in the yard while a crippled cowboy in a hat worn through the crease unloads a brown mare.

You write the cheque and he hands me the lead rope. What's her name? No name.

The rope and halter always go with the horse he says before driving out of our nowhere.

Tyler's First Saddle. Alice surprised Tyler on his seventh birthday at Old Canmore, telling his friends to distract him before leading his horse out with a new saddle.

I look and you say yes. You have bought me a horse of my own. So I could ride anytime. So I could ride anywhere. Anytime. You gave me this. You gave me the mountains and trees and grass and the rising sun and the setting sun. You gave it all to me. A life of my own. I could go anywhere do anything. There is no forgetting the most wonderful yes you ever said. We named her Dolly and she always brought me home.

Don't tell me you are forever locked in the memorial bronze of yesterday. Let my stories be my horse for you. I'll ride Dolly and we'll go everywhere. Anytime.

You showed me how to say yes when that crippled cowboy unloads eternity. That's how much you loved me.

A FAMILY OF SHOW—OFFS

Your birthday again and I'm at Eden Brook for another suitcase visit, this one to tell you I went last week to Montreal to talk to your brother, my Uncle John.

My trip to Montreal will take awhile to explain. When you chose morphine in the Rockyview Hospital, I brought you my first novel, *The Story of Blue Eye*. You smiled with wandering eyes. I signed a copy for you. *To Alice, who taught me how to read, write and ride. Love Tyler.* Where did that copy go? Randy sat by your bed and read excerpts. After the funeral I reread your notes on my first manuscript. Your review. What fun. A mother reviewing her son's book. No wonder you smiled. Your funeral was the day after the book launch. Later that year, *Blue Eye* was nominated for a prize and the finalists were flown to Ottawa. Dad, hoping for gold stars, phoned Uncle John in Montreal. Nobody from the family here is going. Will you? Yes, I will drive to Ottawa. That's where I met John Tyler.

I wonder why you never told me about the Tylers. Another family of strangers. Names mentioned in passing. Big Marjorie. Father Bert. Their children: Little Marjorie born 1921, Alice 1924, Joan 1925, John 1926. All dead now but John. I remember a few years ago you telling me they found Little Marjorie in a hotel apartment. Dead. Who was she? A half-sister you said. I should have asked more questions. Your blue eyes stopped me.

I could have passed Uncle John age 79 on the street and not recognized him.

You named me after him, John Tyler, and called me Tyler. Odd to think I know so little about my namesake.

I brought copies of Your Jens letters to Ottawa. I wanted you there. Uncle John and I chat like airport acquaintances. A nephew and his uncle? He has your familiarity with the crowded gate into AA hell. And the lonely path to redemption. A life traveller in recovery.

He only remembers I liked to ski fast. Long ago. He knows nothing else about me. A writer? That's a surprise to him. A book about the Blackfoot? he asks. Yes. We sit on a couch outside the awards ceremony. He says the crowd inside looks very bookish. Not his type. I like him. I'm not bookish either. He sees through people just like you do. Same challenge in his voice. Don't try to get away with anything. He's bored when the ceremony begins. He's bored while the MC reads the list of finalists and bored while authors read passages from their books. Not real life.

After the awards and handshaking (*Blue Eye* didn't win) he says he has something important to tell me. A family secret about my great-grandmother, Eva Flanagan, Big Marjorie's mother.

A strange time for this, I think.

Eva lived with the Mohawk on the Kahnawake Reserve, he tells me. Maybe that's why you wrote that book about Indians. Did Alice tell you where Eva lived? he asks, and I remember her saying something about her but I wasn't paying attention. It was at the Kellys I remember now in my dishabille suitcase of memories.

It was a slap in the face to our mother, he says. She kept it a secret. I was the only one who visited Eva. Nobody could stop me.

What secrets the Tyler family have. You loved secrets.

I ask about Jens. A Norwegian, he recalls vaguely. A good skier. (Uncle John's kind of real life accomplishment.) Did you know Alice and Jens were engaged? Impossible, he says. Never would have happened. But like you he catches on quickly. He knows there's more to this story. Not bookish stuff. He's interested.

Tell me about my mother.

Suddenly he wants to drive back to Montreal. It is getting late. There will be traffic. No time to tell you about Alice.

We'll talk another time, he promises as he leaves. I sign a book for him. A book about Indians. I wonder if he will read it. He knows more but isn't telling. Yet.

I phone from Calgary. He doesn't say much but he doesn't say he won't help me. I know he doesn't trust me. But not the why of that. By September I have saved enough for a ticket to Montreal and I'm going to see him. He's going to show me Westmount where you lived. Westmount High School. The Alpine Inn. The Tyler family graves. It's a start.

I arrive in a blizzard. He drives with your disregard for the expectation of stop signs and red lights. Hang on. We're going!

Dinner. Then I show him photocopies of the Jens and Alice letters and photographs. They were in love, I tell him.

While he reads, I browse a Tyler family photo album. Not much to see, he warns. Hazel our stepmother took everything when Bert our father died. Hazel the stepmother? It is going to take awhile to sort out these names so I just flip the pages of the album. John Tyler the athlete. Ski team. Hockey team. Could have any girl I guess. Thick dark hair. Portraits of Beautiful Joan. Beautiful Alice. John and Big Marjorie. Little Marjorie. Uncle Ivan. Father Albert. An Albert Edward. An Albert John. No Flanagans. No Eva.

I guess it's true, Uncle John says after he's read Jens's letters. But marriage? No. It never would have happened. Alice never would have married him. He's so sure.

Maybe I missed something. Maybe I wasn't paying attention.

For three days Uncle John drives me around Montreal and the Laurentians. I photograph schools, city homes, summer homes, graves, golf courses, hotels, rivers, and all the while Uncle John slips me pieces of the story. Nobody knows where Eva's buried. Nobody cares.

At first I wonder why he just doesn't start at the beginning and tell it all. Then I realize he too is coming to an understanding. To seeing how extraordinary the Tyler lives were. I make notes twisting arrows across pages to connect names and places. Asterisks. A puzzle of broken threads. I am interpreting chaos.

When Alice was 14 she was already going on 18, Uncle John says. She was way ahead of everybody. He laughs and his eyes are yours, even bluer perhaps. She always had older boyfriends. The O'Brien brothers—Bill and Stuart—Gerry Dakin, Les McClarren, Charles Ronalds, Peter Holt. Some serious. Some to play tennis. She was good at tennis.

"My father's textile business was a bonanza. He started Standard Cottons after he graduated from McGill. His partner was a chartered accountant. They did very well!"

"Very well" is one of Uncle John's favourite expressions. When he uses it, he raises his hands palms out and presses them down slowly in time with his very well. It means that somebody is doing so well that there is no point in even asking how well. Just accept it. Don't ask. I recognize that look.

Uncle John tells me: Big Marjorie—Alice's mother—came to Montreal from Malone in New York State. She was divorced and already had one daughter, Little Marjorie. Three years old. Bert—Alice's father—didn't have it easy, his family and friends snubbed Big Marjorie because she was divorced and had a child. She never forgave them or any of the other society families who looked down on her.

Big Marjorie and Bert are married in 1924. There is always something wrong with Little Marjorie. Unstable, they say. Nervy. The three beautiful children follow quickly.

Bert and Big Marjorie buy a home at 588 Lansdowne Avenue in Westmount—the white only no French no Jews wealthy enclave of Montreal. Maybe Catholic but better to be Anglican. This home is just the start for Big Marjorie. The top of the hill is her aspiration. The mansion at 3803 Westmount Boulevard. The most prominent location.

Big Marjorie is obsessive. Uncle John says she has only one ambition—to stand on the top of Westmount Boulevard and piss down on the people who insulted her when she arrived in Montreal. Not a Canadian Literature image Uncle John.

Her plan begins with raising Alice and Joan as society debutantes. Marry them into the right families and the Tylers will move into high society. Alice and Joan are sent to Miss Edgar's and Miss Cramp's finishing school. There are balls, dinners, coming out parties. High school is all the education a debutante needs to get a husband.

And where was the best place for Big Marjorie's daughters to meet the right men? The Alpine Inn. Owned by the fast moving big money Tyler family. Right in the centre of the Laurentians where the sons and daughters of Westmount's wealthiest families ski play tennis golf and ride horses in preparation for idle lives devoted to spending the interest compounding in grandfather's trust account.

The Tylers build a private lake, summer and winter homes for themselves and their children, guest cottages and stables. Uncle John points them out to me.

I ask about Pierre Trudeau. He was older than Alice, he answers. But they

The Show-Off Life. Big Marjorie and Bert Tyler presided at the Alpine Inn's
"Wings Over Canada" wartime horse show with the Governor General,
the Earl of Athlone, and his wife, Princess Alice (in uniforms).
Photo public domain.

knew each other. She had the brains in our family and was good-looking. She
skied. Of course he would know her.

"We lived a very big life. Our parents were show-offs," he says, getting
back to the family's grand life.

I don't mention the irony of Alice's show-off Country Club exit. What
genealogical tragedy families emulate.

"The Tylers didn't just go to horse shows," he says. "The Tylers had their
own horse shows."

He says all this palms down, so I don't argue with him. A Very Big Life.
I admit I didn't really believe him until I find the Alpine Inn Horse Show
programs and newspaper photos of the Governor General of Canada, the Earl
of Athlone, presiding over the prize giving. Can you guess who is with him?
His wife, Princess Alice! Did you introduce yourself? I also find a newspaper
clipping with photos of Joan and her horse doing very well on the show circuit.

The Alpine Inn had everything: rustic log walls varnished and polished, stone fireplace, 50 rooms, a mezzanine dining room, bar, games rooms, ski shop, beauty salon, tennis courts, stables, guest houses, swimming pool, and a bathhouse.

And the Tyler children were the Inn's royal family. The best of everything. Horses, skis, tennis racquets, cars. Everything.

Uncle John hands me a summary of Alice's Westmount life that he has written. He wants to help and I thank him. Meaning it.

Alice was a poet and writer. She would have loved to be able to be an author. She wrote some poems and many short stories.

Alice was a clever girl and did extremely well in school. She got the acting bug in high school—not unlike Hollywood hopefuls. She was always a very dramatic person. In actual fact this was true to the end of her life. In many ways she was a perfect fit for acting. Very beautiful, great figure, and extra smart way beyond her years. She did some summer theatre with her good friend Betty Goodfellow. They were really never good but it was a lot of fun. And a great way to meet men.

Alice loved men and men loved her. Certainly she was a flirt in many ways. She was never promiscuous.

Alice was beautiful, but alas her sister Joan was more beautiful. Hard for a girl like Alice to swallow but Joan was known as the most beautiful girl in Montreal. Not only that, Joan was a much better athlete. Joan went on to ski for the Canadian National Ski Team. Besides that, Joan was a talented horseback rider and a member of the Quebec Swim team.

Although Joan was younger than Alice she was also no slouch when it came to men.

The Social Scene: Here's a clipping you kept, and now I am keeping for us in Alice's Suitcase. It's a reminder to me that John's story may have sounded like an exaggeration, but it wasn't. It also tells me that despite your rivalry with Joan you could still be proud of her. The article, with photo, describes her as the beautiful Penguin Club racing star and one of the leading contenders for a place on the Eastern Canada Women's Team that will compete at Lake

Two of the Beautiful Tylers. Alice's brother and sister, Joan and John, had everything: formidable athletic ability, good looks, money, and friends.

Placid. To me, the clipping says more about what you chose to keep than it does about Joan's skiing.

Uncle John's summary continues:

Alice had several girlfriends mostly from high school but none of them close. Betty Goodfellow was one. But the truth was Alice was not a girly-girl. She preferred men. She wasn't close to her mother or her sisters. She dearly loved her father...and her brother John.

She loved to dress well and she truly loved coming from a well-to-do family. Maybe she got that from her mother. Once her mother had money, expense was no object. Her mother didn't hesitate to spend money on her girls. She ran up huge charge accounts at Morgan's Department Store.

Maybe the Tyler children were spoiled, but they all had a good life and enjoyed it to the last.

I fold Uncle John's pages, noting how Big Marjorie encouraged the rivalry between her daughters. The winner would be the girl who made the best marriage. Money. Social Position. Approved by Big Marjorie. Her plan.

Uncle John phones Betty Goodfellow. We drive there in the morning for coffee. She's a watercolourist. An artist. A friend to Alice the planning to be writer. As we're talking 1940s Montreal society, Betty politely reminds me that she and John are my godparents.

Now I remember. Betty was the friend who sent you those exquisitely painted Christmas cards each year. One of her cards is in your Eden Brook suitcase. Bundles of her letters. Betty kept most of your letters. You were a wonderful writer, she says. She kept everything. Even your Christmas cards. Beautifully written.

I cannot help smiling when Betty mentions your Christmas cards. Signed in stories that carried onto the back page. I'd watch you at your glass front desk thinking of the addressee then begin to write. Those card wrapped paragraphs still float inside faraway dresser drawers hidden in wonder. Betty remembers them so vividly. Often people tell me they kept your notes and cards.

At first Betty is positive the Jens and Alice engagement isn't true. Alice never mentioned Jens to her. She would have: We were close friends. We talked about...everything! Not a word in her letters. All her life she wrote me about...everything.

I show Betty the letters from Jens. And the photos. She doesn't recognize him. She is a careful and practical thinker. She thinks before saying Alice would never have married somebody like Jens. Besides, it wasn't like Alice to keep a secret of that kind. I was her best friend in Montreal. She would have told me.

Nobody in the family knew, John adds.

I tell them she had once told me she was in love with a pilot. She was drinking. I didn't pay attention. I should have.

Betty frowns then hesitates. She did confide there had been somebody else. It could have been Jens. She didn't tell me who it was. Your mother was a difficult person. Betty says that nicely and I don't need more explanation. I knew Alice's alcoholic flashpoint.

Nobody speaks for a long moment. Then Betty glances at John and back to me. "I remember when your mother got engaged to Ted. She thought her life was going to be wonderful. I told her Ted won't be good for her. She wouldn't listen."

She shakes her head, no, when I ask why she thought Ted would be no good for Alice. "I don't want to say any more about that."

More secrets, I say to myself. Betty is observant. She must have seen or heard something and now she wishes she had told Alice.

Why are you so sure that Alice would not have married Jens? I ask.

Betty lists the reasons on her fingers. In Westmount you chose a man who was:

1) Anglican, or at least a Protestant denomination (Catholic a desperate choice. A status-based system rather than theological),
2) Of British background (American second choice),
3) Educated (university),
4) Had good prospects (family money or a good job), and
5) Not likely to be killed in the war.

Those were the rules in 1940s Westmount Society.

A mother didn't choose a Jens Müller for her daughter to marry.

And if anybody asked the Tyler family about Grandmother Eva, they said she was still living in Malone, New York. None of them knew that old woman living with the Indians on the Kahnawake Reserve. No relation.

It is not until I am landing in Calgary that I wonder, Where did all the Tyler money go?

THE ALPINE INN

At Eden Brook, I am drowsy in the sun. Beside you on the grass my arm over my eyes. I begin to see the too late story of your marlin.

It is December 26, 1940. Jens's first Christmas away from his family. The pilots drove all last night from Little Norway to St. Marguerite's, determined to be skiing as soon as the hill opens. They are staying at the Alpine Inn. He meets Alice in the ski shop. He is buying ski wax when she says, "The red will be the fastest. In an hour the sun will warm the snow and the red will be just right. That is, if you like to go fast."

He nods. "Yes. I like that." Her blue eyes dare him. She tells him where to find the steepest runs. She offers to show him around. They agree to meet for lunch and ski together in the afternoon.

Later that morning on the hill, Jens asks Pilot Officer Ottar Malm about her. He trusts Ottar who has skied here before and knows everybody. Ottar is outgoing. Confident. Gregarious. A natural leader. Her name is Alice Tyler, Ottar says. Her parents own the Alpine Inn. They are rich. They own the golf course. They own businesses in Montreal. They live in Westmount. Very exclusive. She has two sisters and a brother. They are the beautiful Tyler family.

"A Norwegian pilot like you won't have a chance with Alice," Ottar warns but smiles. "She says she's going to McGill University when she finishes school."

"School?" Jens asks. "She looks older than that."

Ottar laughs. "That's why her mother is already making plans for her to marry a rich boy from a proper family. Before some pilot like you comes along and steals her. If you meet her mother you'll know why you don't have a chance."

Jens believes he has a chance. There was something in the way the blue of Alice's eyes brightened when she talked to him. As if the sun flooded the morning sky. He meets her for lunch.

Right away he thinks this conversation is going badly. As usual, he is too serious. Instead of being charming and witty, he talks about the long hours of pilot training. The push to get the pilots into the war. The Battle of Britain. The Luftwaffe versus the Royal Air Force. Dogfights on the horizon. About the plans he had before the war. Studying to be an engineer. About Norway and his motorcycle races. He knows he's making a fool of himself with all these details. He should be flattering her. Complimenting her clothes. Asking about her friends. She seems surprised by his attitude. She seems surprised he would tell her what he thinks about.

It goes better while they are skiing. There's not so much time for him to talk, to make mistakes. She's a determined skier and tries hard to keep up. He admires her bravery. She's not afraid to fall. She's not afraid to make mistakes. She laughs until tears run down her cheeks and he can't help laughing too. He forgets to be serious.

That evening Alice leads him into an office behind the Inn's front desk and closes the door. "This is my father's office. My parents aren't coming up North until New Year's Eve. I study here."

She reaches her arms around his neck, pulling him towards her. "Kiss me, so I know you are real."

Afterwards, she says, "A week isn't very long. I've only known you one day and I am already beginning to miss you."

She is not shy like him. In the dining room she holds his hand as the maître d' leads them to a table. He is self-conscious. His pilot friends are watching.

Her blue eyes pause to rest gently on him. He wishes he knew what she was thinking. Does she think he's just another man hanging around because she's rich? A show-off? Smooth? How can he prove he's different?

They meet again the next day for lunch and skiing. The evening kiss in the office is longer. Her hands around his waist pull his hips into her. At supper they share a table with Ottar and a low neckline redhead from Montreal. Alice's changing eyes are brighter, faster than Jens has ever seen them. She talks excitedly about how her skiing is improving with Jens's help. "Norwegian men know the right techniques," she says. "They have experience." The Montreal girl blushes. Ottar grins.

Alice opens a silver cigarette case. "Can I tempt you, Jens?" she asks.

"I'm not a smoker," he replies.

"Do you have a match?"

He shakes his head, no.

"Pilots should carry matches," she says, "for emergencies." She turns to Ottar to light her cigarette.

"Jens doesn't have temptations or emergencies," Ottar tells her as he strikes a match. "He is the only pilot who helps the mechanics during his free time. The others just lounge about the camp."

"I love temptation," Alice says.

Jens knows he's expected to have a response. He thinks carefully before speaking. "If you make up your own rules, if you live the way you choose, then nothing can tempt you."

Alice rests her cigarette on the glass ashtray and wraps her arms around Jens's neck. "But not everybody can make up their own rules. Not everybody is like you." Then, in his ear, she whispers, "That's why I might love you one day."

He thinks late into the night, lying on his bed while his roommate sleeps drunk twisting in the blankets on the other bed. Could Alice ever love him?

When they meet for lunch the next day, she has brought him a present. "You can open it after skiing today." She tucks a red ribboned box into the pocket of his ski jacket. "I'll meet you in the dining room tonight. Tell me then if you like it."

He's pleased by the gift, but disappointed they won't be meeting in the office for a kiss before supper. He doesn't say anything. The skiing goes well and he thinks about the red ribbon as he rides the lift to the top of the hill. There, he tells her, "I must admit I was tempted to open the box on the way up. Maybe you know me better than I know myself."

"Maybe," she replies.

When the lifts close at dusk, they carry their skis over their shoulders to the racks on the porch of the Inn.

"May I open the gift now?" he asks.

She shakes her head. "After you've had a bath. Then you can open it." She kisses him on the cheek. "I'll see you soon, sweetheart."

He is alone in his room when he unties the red ribbon and opens the box. Inside, resting on a bed of cotton wool, is a box of matches. "I Am Your Emergency."

BEFORE THE FORGETTING CAME

As I read The Jens Album, our 13 years of Goodbye Mother memories begin to find me. I write them as they find me and read them aloud to you at Eden Brook. This is the first.

Old Canmore, and our cabin there, wasn't much. Everything was black and dying in that 1950s coal town except the Three Sisters mountains, the Bow River, and the wind scattering shadows beneath the spruce.

For me, the best thing that happened at Canmore was nothing. I did everything inside nothing. Everything I wanted to do or know was in the nothingness I lived.

The main street was a few old low roofed dirt floored shacks, cracked sidewalks, a fight and spit hotel bar, the RCMP jail, a barber shop, and Leong's grocery and coffee shop.

I was an unnoticed little kid and did what I wanted. Nobody said anything, or cared, as long as I stayed away from the bar.

Mary Anderson and I saved pop bottles and exchanged six empties at Leong's for a full one. Leong's had wood floors, black and slippery from years of coal dust ground into them by miners' boots. If we had five empties we had to drink the full one on the steps and return the empty right away. Mary figured out the best deals on liquorice, gum, jawbreakers. She was alive in the nothingness of summer and so was I.

The barber shop had one chair and one haircut for boys. A pig shave. I rode Dolly there once a month and when I got home you rinsed my bald head with coal oil to get rid of the bugs.

The mine railway ran on the edge of the town. On the cabin side of the tracks was the miners' golf course, nine holes with oiled sand greens. Our cabin was beside a green. Geoff—two years younger—and I played rounds of golf with one ball and one club each for driving and putting. I chose your two iron. Geoff was always the best at sports and could beat me with any club. The golf course was also good pasture for hobbled or picketed horses.

Our cabin was a shack. Plywood walls sided with half logs. A Bow River stone fireplace built around a Heatilator metal box banked with coal at night. Where your nightie caught on fire and Aunt Joanie rolled you in the rug to put it out. Both drunk.

Across the flat from us were the Firmstones and the Andersons. Duncan Crockford, the Scottish landscape painter, lived on the hill above the Rundle Mountain Trading Company Store and the Canmore Coal Company Headquarters. It wasn't until I read Henry Miller's *Tropic of Cancer* that I understood why you loved these people so much. First there were the quick snorts. The sudsy ones. The before and after dinner ones. The nightcaps. Finally, the ones for the road. I'd be burrowed into a corner listening as the bottles piled up on the kitchen counter. Helen Firmstone was the sharpest and forever a good friend to you. Her father was Harry Pollard who carried his photograph equipment from the Rockies to the pharaohs' tombs.

Helen was as hardy as her father and the only person I know who could put her arms around me and I didn't feel like crying before the forgetting came. The drinking just about killed her husband Gary but he kept up.

Like Dad, Dr. Anderson wasn't around much (for different reasons) but Hilda and their girls were. Hilda played the banjo and the girls all sang and I was astounded. The older Anderson girls had boyfriends hanging around. They took us to the flickering movies in the Canmore Opera House and carried us on their shoulders home asleep and safe over the Bow River trestle. Hilda sunned in her bra at lunchtime on our mountain hikes.

And into the cabin the screen door shoved aside would roar Duncan Crockford his Scottish accent rolling through his thick beard and bad teeth. His wife Wynn urging him to get back to his painting. Impossible. He had money today. Duncan crashed through life painting and womanizing. His eye always wandering to you. Teasing English accent Ted. The office man. I'd see Duncan later unmistakable in his kilt seducing businessmen's bored wives at the symphony art auctions.

The overcrowded cabin of laughter and flames was your drowning time with Henry Miller in Montmartre. Your brawl with Ernest in Havana. The coal grime, everyone pissing behind the cars, the Rockies and Bow River painted by Duncan. This was your life of *New Yorker* stories. The nowhere time of Canmore cold water showers and bottles of gin stories ready for mailing.

I remember knowing for the first time I was loved. It didn't happen fast. Probably over a summer or even over a couple of years. I was five when I noticed it, 1954.

I remember standing on the plywood porch of the bunkhouse. The nothingness of the morning quiet. Pine and spruce smells flowing like water around me. The smell of my nothingness. The sun flickering on silk centred cobwebs in the bush.

I always wore a T-shirt and blue jeans with rolled up cuffs. Unless it was cold. Then I wore my dark red flannel shirt with gold horseshoes and silver lariats. Most cowboy shirts had pearl snaps. Mine had plain white buttons. The cuffs and elbows were fraying and I pulled the loose threads off. I was tidy. I tucked the silver tip of my belt into the loops of my jeans. The belt had a turquoise bead pattern on the back. Some cowboys I had seen at the McBride corrals had brands stamped on their belts. Some cowboys wore knives on their belts. I kept mine in my pocket. It wasn't very big.

I always wore sneakers. Tennis shoes. They were best because you never knew what you might be doing that day. Boots were too hot and no good for running or in the water. Men wore boots. I lived to be ready for anything.

My brothers were sleeping in the bunks, their blankets pulled around their heads. It was cold in the mountains at night. They didn't like me to wake them. They liked sleeping. I liked being alone in the morning and wandering around. I went to the corrals first to feed the horses from a big stack of bales beside the corral. I had fed the last of a bale the night before, so I had to climb to the top of the stack and roll one free. It bounced to the ground. The horses pushed against the rails as I cut the strings and hung them on a fence post. They were useful when rails came off the corral. I couldn't pound the big nails.

The best horses that summer were Twinkle, Trixie, and Belle. Other horses came and went. Apache who always rolled when I rode him into a creek. The saddle got wet and unless I was quick to jump to the bank I got wet too. Red who could gallop on hobbles so Mum had to be careful when she let him out to graze.

I threw the hay flakes into the corral, spreading them out so all the horses got enough. I couldn't ride Belle until she had finished eating but I could sit on her. The only way I could get on was to take her hay to the corral fence and push her tight against a rail. Before she moved away I had to run behind her, crawl through the rails, climb to the top, and swing a leg over her back. Sometimes it took two or three tries. I sat on her while the horses ate the hay. Until they started biting and kicking each other, fighting over the last flakes.

I slid off and got my rope halter. I stood on a log to put it over Belle's head. I had to slide the halter's stiff loop through a keeper and bend it onto a hook. I took my chances with being safe and just tugged the loop over the hook. I led her from the corral and brushed her. I would have saddled her but that took time. Yesterday it took so long I got stopped riding past the cabin and had to go inside and eat breakfast. Better to eat first. Then ride.

The buzzing of flies grew from the quiet. Belle swished her black tail. The sun was warm and all around the clearing were the tall emerald trees and above them a circle of leaning mountains. The brush slid over Belle's coat. I had nothing else to do but stand in the bottom of that morning cup of sky blue life and brush my horse. That was forever made wordless real and nothing to talk about.

I knew Mum was awake now. I led Belle back to the corral and walked along the path to the cabin. Scuffed roots crossed the path. Between the roots the dirt was low and hard and rust red pine needles drifted in the dips. My fingers trailed through the branches pulling fresh needles. I stopped at the door and held my hands against my face, washing with the smell of broken emeralds.

Geoffrey in his flannel pyjamas stood on a chair at the table banging a spoon on the edge of his bowl. He splashed the spoon into his glass of milk and laughed as the milk splattered over his hand. Teddy the biggest of us sat at the end of the table cutting toast. He was setting an example and had his hair brushed and was sitting up straight.

Billy was in the high chair. He smeared his pablum over his face and licked it from his hands then reached toward Geoffrey's bowl.

"Bake," Geoffrey shouted as he smacked his spoon on the table. "Bake."

"Do you want bacon?" she asked me.

"Bake," Geoffrey shouted again.

"I want some," Teddy said. He looked at me with his four years older than you brushed hair. "Daddy's coming for the weekend. Today is Friday." As if I didn't know. Anything.

I sank into her big reading chair by the fireplace and flipped my legs over the arm. I reached down and lifted up a pile of her *New Yorker*s. She read them at night. I knew she was watching me as I turned the pages looking for cartoons.

"Do you want toast and jam?" she asked.

"Bake," Geoffrey demanded. He slammed his spoon on the table. "Bake."

Brown toast. Butter. Strawberry jam. Bacon. That was breakfast. That was always breakfast and sometimes lunch. The propane stove whoomped as she lit the burner.

Teddy made more toast. She fried the bacon and piled it on a plate in the centre of the table beside the can of strawberry jam that said With Pectin. What was that? Nobody ever asked for the jam with pectin.

Geoffrey waved his slice of bacon in the air. "Bake."

Billy cried until she gave him a slice. Teddy used his knife and fork to cut his bacon. I layered mine. Toast, jam with pectin, bacon, toast.

I squished my sandwich so I could pull the bacon apart with my teeth.

"Daddy's coming today," Teddy said. Again. He was good at chewing with his mouth closed.

"Yes," she said. "We're going to have a quiet day. Teddy's going to work on his reading and arithmetic and we're going to be quiet for him."

"What's pectin?" I asked.

She liked being caught by my guess where to look questions. "We don't know what pectin is," she said with her eyes laughing only with me. "You tell us."

I turned the can towards her and pointed to the word. "Pectin. What is it?"

Teddy pulled the can from my hands and read the label out loud. "Strawberry Jam With Pectin." He frowned, then smiled. "It's what's in the jam. That's what it says."

I looked at her and she was biting her bottom lip. "That's what pectin is," she said. "Teddy's right. It's what's in the jam."

"Bake," Geoffrey shouted as he crawled onto the table and tipped over the bacon plate.

Teddy and I piled the dishes in the sink and she washed Geoffrey and Billy. "Play together," she said to Geoffrey as she set Billy on the floor. Geoffrey climbed back onto his chair and chanted, "Wanna go in the car! Gotta go in the car!" He slammed his hands on the table.

She lifted him from the table and set him on the floor to play with Billy. "Wanna go in the car! Gotta go in the car!"

Billy waved his hands then began to cry when Geoffrey stood up and climbed the chair.

"Get your books," she said to Teddy.

"I'm going riding," I said as I stepped over Billy.

"That's not fair. Tyler should do school work too," Teddy said. "He should have something to show Daddy when he gets here."

"I can't read," I said. "I'm not in school."

Teddy and Alice laughed. Together. Family.

She came to the corral and saw me standing small on a bale straining to tighten the cinch on Belle.

She wrapped her arms around me. It was like the emerald trees and the leaning mountains wrapping themselves around me. Blue eyes like the top of the cup. Only the smell was different. She smelled like bacon.

"Do you need help?" she asked.

"It's tight."

"I have to stay with the boys."

"I know. Daddy is coming."

Suddenly her hands were strong around my waist and she swung me laughing shoes high into the saddle.

"Don't fall off or you'll have to walk home."

"I won't."

"I love you."

I was her you. I lived. Wrapped inside the blue eyed sky bacon sandwich love of her nothingness.

NEW YEAR'S EVE 1941

Conquering Nazis parade in Oslo. In the snow-covered Laurentians of Quebec, Canada, Jens Müller and four other Norwegian pilots have made the most of their one week leave. Pilots in exile. All week they competed with the Canadian men for the fastest run on the ski hill. They built a ski jump, the first on the hill. Daredevils, the Canadians said.

At night, the competition was in the dining room and bar of the Alpine Inn. For the girls. The Norwegians in uniform had the advantage. New. Exciting. Different.

Jens has not noticed the way the girls' eyes follow him on the ski hill, or now, as he stands alone in a corner of the Inn watching the New Year crowd. As usual, he is keeping to himself. The other pilots tease him about his solemn attitude.

The Inn's varnished log walls glisten with light crackling from the tall stone fireplace. In the balcony above the dining room, a four-piece band plays slow tunes. The rafters appear to sway as red and green streamers unwind in the rising heat. Montreal socialites chat over a white wine supper. The husbands wear tuxedos with crisp white shirts. The wives wear stiff dark gowns with high necks and low hems.

New Year's Eve is passing slowly for Jens. After spending almost the whole week with Alice, he is going to spend the last night of his leave alone.

She had warned him. Her parents were coming to the Inn. She would have to sit with them. He won't have her to himself.

"But it will be my last night here. Our last night together."

Jens's Norton. This photo of the heroic and handsome Jens on his motorcycle would have thrilled the adventurous Alice while giving Big Marjorie social nightmares. Photo courtesy of Jon Müller.

"I can't help it. My mother insists I sit with her. It is family. I have no choice."

You do, he thought but did not say.

He has been preparing himself all day for this evening, knowing it wasn't going to be easy watching Alice from a distance. He is doing a good job of keeping his thoughts under control.

He should be enjoying his last day of leave so he can train harder when he returns to camp. He needs to work more on his navigation. Studying navigation is important, not just for a fighter pilot, but for a commercial pilot after the war. Everything is important, damn it. He mustn't let himself get distracted by a girl he has known for less than a week. Alice Tyler.

The war is in its second year. If he is to survive, he must learn all he can before he joins the British squadrons.

He will not allow himself to think about his mother and brother under the eyes of the Nazis. He will not allow himself to think about his father in a Chinese prison. He will not think about the friends he lost when the Nazis invaded. He will not think of the engineering studies he left in Zurich. He will not think about his Norton motorcycle and the Oslo summer races.

He will only think about flying.

He will not think about his dash from Zurich to Bordeaux and then to London where he enlisted in the Royal Norwegian Air Force. He had worried unnecessarily about being accepted. That was a lesson to remember. Don't worry unnecessarily. The Government in Exile examiners hadn't questioned his ability to complete the training. He'd been flying since he was 18. That was for fun. The thrill. That was yesterday. This is for war. Hurricanes. Spitfires. Focke-Wulfs. Now he must concentrate on surviving the war as a fighter pilot. His home now is Little Norway, the training camp outside Toronto.

Stay in control of your thoughts. That's the way to survive. His Norton ran perfectly. Always. He planned his races carefully, leaving as little as possible to chance. Like the day he roared the motorcycle run full speed down the mountainside between two tramlines. He'd sat on the top of the mountain for hours watching the trams go up and down, passing each other near the middle. His friends bet him he couldn't ride between the passing trams.

He watches and plans. Then, when he sees the moment, he kicks the motor over and roars down the mountainside. The trams flash by on either side. Only his thoughts run slowly. Always under control.

At the bottom he collects the bet. I knew it could be done, he says. I'm not a daredevil.

Tonight, he promises himself, he will celebrate like the other pilots. This is New Year's Eve. I will enjoy it, even if I have to pretend that I am only living for today. The future is nothing. Planes crash. Planes are shot down. Why worry? Make the most of every opportunity.

And he will not think about the 15-hour drive home tomorrow. Tonight he will celebrate the great skiing. The freedom.

He allows himself one hope. Perhaps he will have a chance to be alone with Alice. To see her eyes turn blue soft. The winter sky above Oslo.

Ottar is right. A girl like Alice expects more than I can offer. Ottar knows about these Canadians. Who am I? No education. No money. A foreigner.

A fighter pilot who probably won't live through the war. No prospects. It is a mistake to get serious about a girl I may never see again. And look at her now, laughing and flirting with the men standing around her parents' table. She can take her pick.

"Where's your poker face tonight?" Ottar asks. "It looks to me like you're breaking your heart over that Tyler girl."

"I have a chance with her," Jens replies. "Her parents are the problem."

"Of course they are," Ottar says. "They know pilots fly away and never come back. No matter what they promise."

"If I say I'll come back, I will."

Ottar laughs. "Got it all planned out, don't you?" He sets his glass on the bar. "Come with me. I'll introduce you to her parents. Then you'll know who you're up against. Big Marjorie. She's the boss. Just call her Mrs. Tyler and you'll do fine. Alice's father is Bert. Everybody likes him."

Big Marjorie is small. Maybe five feet. Dark-haired with low lid hazel eyes that study Jens. A Panzer gunner choosing a target. Are you armed, her eyes ask? No matter. I am the Blitzkrieg. Unstoppable.

"This is Second Lieutenant Jens Müller," Ottar says, pulling a chair from another table to sit beside Big Marjorie.

Bert stubs out a cigarette, pours himself two inches of Scotch, drinks it, then stands and shakes Jens's hand. "Pleased to meet you. Any friend of Ottar Malm's is a friend of the Tyler family. He's charmed all of Montreal. Even Mrs. Tyler and she's damned hard to charm."

Blue eyes, Jens thinks about Bert. Like Alice. An athlete. Getting heavy.

"Jens is our best pilot," Ottar says. "And best skier. He'll be racing for Norway at the military competitions in February. He's been helping Alice."

Alice smiles at Jens. "Yes, he has," she tells her mother. "Jens has very good technique."

Big Marjorie ignores Alice. "Do you speak English?" she asks Jens. Identify yourself.

"Yes, Mrs. Tyler," he answers. "My father was an engineer in Shanghai. I was born there and studied English in school." Big Marjorie is already looking away. Jens is of no consequence. A nobody in Montreal. She watches the maitre d' seat a family near the dance floor. She whispers to Bert who shrugs.

Jens is still standing beside the table, not sure whether he should stay or leave.

Big Marjorie looks up at him. "Well, good luck with your war," she says then turns to Alice. "I have a wonderful evening planned for you, darling. You have a partner for every dance."

Ottar slides his chair back and stands. "I think I'd better buy Jens a drink. We have a long night and drive ahead of us. Enjoy your evening, Mr. and Mrs. Tyler."

"Have a good time, boys," Bert says as they leave the table. "Tell the bartender your next round is on me."

At the bar, Ottar clinks glasses with Jens. "There's nothing you can do. Big Marjorie keeps a close eye on Alice. I wouldn't be surprised if she's already picked the man Alice will marry. I know she's been working on a university fellow named Don."

Jens gulps down his drink and sets the glass down hard on the bar. "Damn it. I wanted Alice to have a good time tonight. She shouldn't have to sit with her parents and dance with whoever they choose. She's got a mind of her own."

"You really are in love with her, aren't you?"

"I am."

Ottar grins. "I never thought I'd see you show your feelings about anything."

"You don't have to worry. This won't affect my flying."

"It might," Ottar says. "Especially after you see me dancing with Alice tonight."

"You!"

"That's right. Big Marjorie has given me a waltz with Alice. She thinks I'm a safe choice. But here's what I'm going to do. Just before eleven o'clock the band will take a break. The first dance after that is supposed to be my waltz. You can have it, instead of me."

Jens shakes his head. "I can't ask you to do that for me."

"It's my duty. You're my best pilot and it's my responsibility that you return to training camp ready to fly. I don't want you crashing because your heart is broken."

"What about Big Marjorie? She won't like this."

"I can handle Big Marjorie. I come from a family with money. That counts with her. I'll be forgiven if Alice has one dance with a Shanghai Norwegian pilot. Besides, I know Alice. I can tell she's fallen for you. This way I'm helping two friends."

After the break, Jens waits until the Tylers have sat down at their table before asking Alice to dance.

"I'm sorry," Big Marjorie interrupts. "Alice has promised this waltz to Pilot Officer Malm."

"Pilot Officer Malm sends his regrets. He has asked me to take his place."

"I'm sorry, that's impossible. I have given our neighbour's son, Donald, the privilege of being the first stand-in."

Jens continues to stand beside Alice. "Perhaps Alice could choose," he says. "Perhaps she would accept me as the stand-in for this waltz."

Big Marjorie frowns. "Well, Alice. What's your choice? Donald or this Norwegian pilot?"

Alice's eyes are dull when she answers. "If it was already decided, then it should be Donald."

The band plays "Auld Lang Syne" at midnight and champagne corks pop. Jens drifts through the bar wishing his pilot friends a Happy New Year. On his way outside for fresh air he sees Alice tying her boots on the porch. He turns away, knowing he might slip. Might reveal his disappointment.

"Jens," she calls out gently. "Come here. Please." She stands on one of the benches, arms around his neck, and whispers, "Be patient." Moments later, Big Marjorie is there and leads her to their car.

His friends are too hungover in the morning to drive. Some sleep while Jens drives. The others barely murmur as he slides the car around an icy corner. He will write Alice a letter as soon as he is back in camp.

"But I won't let this affect my flying. I won't be foolish."

FALLING IN LOVE

After Jens returned to Little Norway to resume training and Alice returned to Montreal, they began writing each other. All I had to guide me in understanding their love was the Jens letters Alice pasted in her album.

Reading Jens's letters had two effects on me. First, I kept hoping for him, that he would be able to keep his promises to Alice. Second, the letters helped me remember the mother of my childhood. In Jens's letters I could see he knew that Alice was much more than a debutante—much more. For the first time since our railway station goodbye, I was sure Jens had known the same Alice that I had.

His letters helped me roll the stone from my forgetting place.

January 26, 1941

Dear Alice,

It really is difficult finding the words to express my feelings when receiving and reading your letters. In Norwegian I think I could, or if I had some of your ability to write. The only thing I can say is that you're wonderful Alice.

I'm so glad to hear you got that part. You seem to be very serious about becoming an actress. If you are able to criticize your own ability and results in the acting business, and you really think you're good, I would take the chance and go in for it, although it seems to be hard competition nowadays. Hope to get a chance to see you in that play. Good luck to you!

"Better luck next time," Alice wrote to Jens with her typical never give up attitude after he crashed this Fairchild PT-26 Cornell in training outside Toronto.

The last days have not at all been dull here. Specially one event has changed my plans for the near future a great deal. — Here's what happened. I was out on a navigation trip in a Fairchild trainer. After one hour of flying I suppose I got in a "playful mood" and dived down on a river. I flew along this some minutes about 4.5 feet above the water. Coming around a bend, in between the high banks, I flew under a telephone wire going across the river. The wire peeled the rudder and tin off the plane. Nearly without any control the plane now headed towards the trees on the bank. I pulled up above them, cut the motor, and the plane sat down among the trees. It didn't stop till we hit the ground, but then it stopped. The plane was a complete wreck, and I should have been too, but I was lucky as usual. I remember having read some-where that "every landing one can walk away from is a good landing". Well, the "boss" didn't seem to know that, so the result of the whole thing is that I most probably will have to go to jail for 30 days. Well, that's that. It was fun while it lasted, but it "ain't no more"! About that trip to England, I suppose it'll still be within reach. Of all the things to do I had to crash a plane at a time where a happening much less serious than that could spoil everything. Well it's no use sitting down and being sad. — One thing is sure, hearing from you Alice, at this time means if possible more to me than usual.

The good thing about the whole affair is that they probably will give me a last chance to see my friends before I go to jail (very Tragic?!) So I think I'll get leave this weekend, which means leaving here Friday at 6 in the evening, arriving Montreal about 3 in the night! As I really think it would be a pity waking you up at this time of the night, I'd better call on you at about 10? I'll phone you before I leave here, provided you have given me the "all clear", and it won't collide with your other engagements.

Sunday we went up to Bethany near Peterborough to train for the competition at Huntsville next Sunday. We had a really good day of skiing. Ottar was photographed by the press, with a whole bunch of sweet girls of course.

Well Alice, I'll be seeing you. In the mean time, send a letter, will you? Ottar sends his best greetings to you all, and so do I.

Jens

Undated Draft

Dear Jens,

Sorry to hear about your accident. What — or who — were you thinking about! Better luck next time. Please telephone the moment you arrive. I shall be waiting to hear from you. Don't wait till ten o'clock. I will not be in until two thirty Saturday morning anyhow so it won't make any difference if I stay up another half hour.

February 5, 1941

Dear, dear Alice

Well, today they read the punishment I got for that crash: 30 days and $50 fine. I'll have to stay in jail only outside the service time. That means I'll be flying just as much as before. And I'll be able to sport too. The worst part is not getting a chance to see you again. So now you have a[n] opportunity of doing some war work. You will keep a "pilot" alive by writing often.—The boys here are a swell lot. Two hours after I got the fine they had gathered together the fifty dollars and paid it. I really felt shameful, as the crash was due to the very bad piloting of me, and I deserved every bit of that punishment.

You seem to be a very busy young lady nowadays. I don't see how you can possibly manage all you do. You'll wear yourself completely out by studying so late. Suppose it'll be better when the examinations are over though. Good luck! We've had two examinations here to but in this outfit we take that sort of thing very lightly.

Alice, we won't be seeing each other for another month after all. I only hope the time won't change things too much Alice?

February 12, 1941

Dear, dear Alice...

Thanks so much for your letter today again...And will I wear your school pin! What a question. Now it's on my flying helmet, and there it shall stay till I'm through with flying....

Jens

Undated Draft

Hello there darling,

I felt so lost when I didn't hear from you Friday and that is why I am writing to tell you how much you mean to me darling. The three days you have been away feel like three years.

I love you with all my heart.

Alice

(By the way, I see I've been editing out a lot of chit-chat from the letters you received from Jens, your family, and your friends. As you must have been, I am intrigued by Poker Face who is turning out to be surprisingly communicative when it comes to writing about his love for you. With that intent so obvious I am leaving untouched the idiosyncrasies of everyone's spelling and punctuation.)

April 7, 1941

Dearest!

You should hear the boys: "What! You're not married?" "And not even engaged?!" And they were really sincere about it. I certainly must have looked as if I were in love when I left for Montreal. It's funny because they used to call me "poker-face" in Norway.

As the lights will go out very soon I have to close now, although I hate to stop writing you. You seem to be so close Alice, sometimes, I can hear you whisper "I love you" quite clearly.

Till tomorrow.

With all my heart I love you, and I'll always be yours

Jens

A NIGHT OUT WITH BIG MARJORIE

Windsor Station, Montreal, 1941

"This will warm you up, Blondie," Bert says as he splashes whiskey from a silver flask into their coffee mugs. "It's damn near as cold in here as it is outside."

"I'm okay, Dad. I'm worried about Mother. If the train isn't here in the next ten minutes I'll have to phone the restaurant and tell her we'll be late."

"I'd better phone," Bert says. "Not you. I'll tell the maitre d' to open a bottle of wine. That will keep her busy until we get there."

"But the doctor told her—" Alice begins.

"I know what the doctor told her," Bert interrupts. "But if Mother sits alone in the restaurant without a drink, she'll cause more trouble than she will with a bottle of wine."

They wait, sipping their coffee and not talking. Uniformed soldiers are slouched on the benches, their legs stretched over dark green duffle bags. A few of the soldiers have brought their girlfriends to the station to say goodbye.

Alice watches one of the girls crying onto a soldier's chest. This war is nothing but hellos and goodbyes.

A whistle blasts across the platform and into the waiting room. Alice feels the floor tremble. The soldiers sit up.

"The train's coming!" Alice says to Bert. "I'm going outside." She hands him her empty mug and is the first through the door.

Jens jumps from the coasting train, a leather bag over his shoulder. With his free arm he scoops up Alice and swings her to his side, her feet arcing weightlessly above the platform.

Bert watches through the window and frowns.

Inside the waiting room, Jens shakes Bert's hand and says, "It is a pleasure to see you again, Mr. Tyler."

"Call me Bert. We'd better hurry. Mrs. Tyler is waiting at the restaurant. I'll get a taxi. I hope that's the only luggage you have."

"Yes. This is everything." Jens lifts the bag onto his shoulder. "I changed into my dress uniform on the train so I'd be ready to go to the restaurant."

"Allez!" Bert orders the driver.

The maitre d' is waiting at the door. "Monsieur Tyler!" he says with a slight bow. "At last you have arrived. You had perhaps a little delay at the station?"

Bert hands him a folded bill. "The train was late. But we're here now and we're hungry. I hope your chef has something special for us. My little Blondie wants to make a big impression on her friend."

The maitre d' scans Jens and smiles. "Tall and debonair. Army?"

Jens shakes his head. "Air Force. Norwegian."

The maitre d' nods in approval. "A pilot! Très gallant. Perhaps one day you will be able to return to your homeland."

Très gallant and très handsome, Alice thinks. He'd better return to me.

The maitre d' turns to Bert who says, "Thank you for taking care of Mrs. Tyler."

"My honour. Mrs. Tyler and her dinner companion have been amusing themselves with la petite Gertrude."

"Her dinner companion?" Alice asks Bert. "I thought it was just the four of us this evening."

"We'll see," Bert answers as he takes her arm and they follow the maitre d' to an alcove in the back of the dining room.

Big Marjorie is sitting at the end of the table. On her right is a formally dressed man in his early twenties. On a small table beside him a piglet sucks milk from a baby bottle held by Big Marjorie.

Bert leans over and kisses Big Marjorie's cheek. Over his shoulder, her expressionless hazel eyes study Jens.

"Sorry we're late, my dear," Bert apologizes. "The train from Toronto was delayed. Something to do with troop departures."

"Graham and I didn't mind waiting, did we? Gertrude has been amusing us. Another half hour and she might have been fat enough to be our supper tonight!"

The young man stands as Big Marjorie introduces him. "Bert, you remember Graham Morton, don't you? The son of Henry and Babs. I asked him to join us this evening, so we'd have company if the train failed to arrive. Everything about the military is unreliable these days."

Graham shakes Bert's hand. "My parents speak highly of you and Mrs. Tyler. And, of course, your exquisite daughter." He smiles at Alice and delicately shakes her hand. "Your mother mentioned you are considering McGill. I'm in second year accounting there. Perhaps one day you would allow me to introduce you around. It's important to meet the right crowd."

Mother has picked a smooth bastard to ruin the evening, Alice thinks.

"Perhaps," Alice replies and turns to Jens. "Graham, this is Second Lieutenant Jens Müller. He's training with the Norwegian pilots outside Toronto."

Graham shakes Jens's hand enthusiastically. "Ah. The famous skiers. Heard all about you chaps from my pals up North. Not a skier myself. Tricky knee. A climbing accident. Put me out of the war game too. Worst luck. Golf's the only action I see these days."

"Gentlemen," Big Marjorie interrupts. "Please sit so we can all talk. I'd like Bert at the other end of the table and Alice on Bert's right. Graham will stay on my left, and Jens will sit on my right." She pronounces his name with a hard *J*.

"Mother," Alice interrupts. "It's pronounced *Yens*. Not *Jens*."

Graham holds Alice's chair and slides it under her as she sits.

"Now then," Big Marjorie says. "I suggest we all begin with a glass of the red wine that Graham and I started before you arrived. We've been having such a delightful time we've barely had time to taste it."

The maitre d' opens a second bottle and circles the table pouring.

Big Marjorie faces Jens and holds her hand over his. "Now, tell me Jens, would you like to feed Gertrude? Or is that not a custom you have yet developed in your country?" Again, she pronounces his name with a hard *J*.

He meets her eyes. "If that is the custom here, I should like to try." He reaches across the table and holds the bottle while the piglet sucks.

Alice claps her hands lightly and says, "Well done, Jens. Now let me have a turn."

As Alice is holding the bottle, the restaurant photographer steps into the alcove. "May I take a complementary photograph of your daughter with Gertrude?" he asks Big Marjorie.

"Only if you promise to display it prominently," she answers. Graham hands Gertrude to Alice who holds her for the photographer as if she were feeding a baby. Two waiters carry Gertrude into the dining room where other guests are photographed with her.

"Would anyone care for a cigarette?" Graham asks as he opens a gold case. "How about you Alice?"

"I'll save that temptation for another time," she replies. "Jens is always talking about self control and I'd like to show him I have it, too."

"Good for you Blondie," Bert says. "The Tyler family has never had much self control."

"Nonsense!" Big Marjorie snaps. "Life is dismal enough without feeling guilty about a few pleasures. I'll have one of your cigarettes Graham."

Graham pulls two cigarettes from under a thin gold spring in his case. Just as he hands one to Big Marjorie, Jens opens the box of matches Alice had given him.

"Allow me," he says as he strikes one and holds it for Big Marjorie.

"Let's order," Bert says. "Jens must be starving after the train ride. I don't suppose they offer much on the troop trains. I want to give him a real Montreal meal so he'll have good memories of Canada while he's shooting down the Luftwaffe. Where are the menus?"

"There is no need for menus," Big Marjorie says. "When I rightly anticipated the train would be late, I ordered a special meal for everybody so it would be ready when you arrived. We're going to share two Gertrudes this evening. The chef has them roasting. He promised me they'd be ready by 7:30. So we have an opportunity to talk and hear more about our guests. Graham can begin by telling us about his plans after McGill." She turns to Jens. "I won't ask your plans. We can't expect pilots to have plans for after the war."

You goddamn bitch, Alice thinks.

Graham talks about university and his father's investment business until the waiter interrupts to say the roast piglets are ready.

"Nicely spoken, Graham," Big Marjorie says while the waiters carry the trays to the table. "You certainly have your life thoroughly planned. When this war is over your father's firm should do quite well with their investments. Bert and I have been doing splendidly with our textile business. We were clever getting our Celanese contract before those fools in government started controlling prices. Otherwise, the war might have proven less to our advantage."

Graham nods in agreement. "The Tyler family is a fine example to my generation."

Bert taps his fork against his glass. "In honour of Jens's upcoming departure from Canada and the dangers he will face, I think it would be appropriate if we asked him to give the blessing for this meal."

Oh, no, Alice thinks. Now there's going to be trouble.

Everybody is looking at Jens who says, "I cannot give a blessing. I am not a believer, Mr. Tyler."

Big Marjorie gasps, her hand at her throat.

"Allow me the privilege," Graham offers before Big Marjorie can speak. "Would you like it in Latin or in English, Mr. Tyler?"

"English will do," Bert replies.

"Our Father. We thank You for this food and the life it brings us. In Your name we ask You to bless this food and make us worthy to do Your will. In Your name we also ask You to bless the Tyler family for their generosity in raising funds at their annual horse show and community events for the brave men who are fighting for our country. Amen."

"Well done, Graham," Big Marjorie says patting his hand.

The waiters carve and serve the piglets, leaving the apple stuffed heads on the trays.

"Now it is your turn, Jens," Big Marjorie says. "Tell us about life in Norway."

You goddamn bitch, Alice thinks again. More trouble. If he tells her about his motorcycle racing, we're both doomed.

For the first time that evening Jens smiles. He folds his napkin and sets it beside his plate. "First, I must tell you I have one plan for after the war. I will return to Canada."

I hope so, Alice thinks.

"What about your family?" Big Marjorie asks. "Won't they expect you to return to Norway?"

The smile leaves Jens's face. "The last I heard, my father is a prisoner in China. I have not heard from my mother and brother since the Nazis occupied Norway." Jens lifts his wineglass. "To happier times. Now, Mrs. Tyler, it is your turn. Tell us about your life. Alice is always saying how interesting your life has been."

"How sweet of my daughter to say that about me. I must admit I wonder occasionally if she appreciates all I do in her best interest?"

"Tell Jens about New York," Bert urges. "About the convent in Malone."

"That's not a cheerful story," she replies.

"Please, Mrs. Tyler," Jens says. "There must be some cheerfulness in it. Look at the marvellous life you have now. I am sure your account will give me many pleasant memories to take overseas."

Nothing my mother loves more than talking about herself, Alice thinks.

Big Marjorie studies her watch. "This may take more than a few minutes. Graham, will you be terribly disappointed if we missed the wrestling at the Forum?"

"Whatever you want, Mrs. Tyler. Or we can go another evening. I'm as curious as Jens about your life. My parents speak so often about your parties and good work in Montreal that I never considered until now your life as a child. I am sure it is fascinating."

Big Marjorie snaps her fingers at a passing waiter. "A bottle of Scotch. Pour me a double and leave the bottle. We're going to need it tonight."

Under the table, Alice slips off her shoe and slides her toes over Jens's ankle. He doesn't change expression. Poker Face, she thinks.

"WE ARE GOING TO GET MARRIED . . ."

In June 1941, the first RNAF squadron of fighter pilots, including Second Lieutenant Jens Müller #125, flies across the Atlantic to join the British air defence. Jens writes Alice from the last refuelling stop in Canada, wondering if she has told her mother about their engagement... the promise he reminded her of but knew would be hard for her to keep.

June 1941

Dearest!

Heaven only knows when you will receive this, and when I'll hear from you.

Since we left the camp and Toronto I've been able to center my mind and thoughts more clearly on you and me and the future. The only thing that really matters though, had never left my thoughts: we love each other and are going to get married as soon as this war makes it possible. Alice dear, you have no idea how much I've missed you and will miss you till we meet again. However, the training and service I've got ahead of me, will require all my ability and concentration so I guess the time will fly anyhow. Besides I can not imagine this war will last the year out.

For the first time in a couple of years I've got time to read, which I'm doing all day. I hope I'll get time in England. By the way, how about the "Readers Digest" you promised me?

The first days of this trip has been rather dull but we got a good deal more excitement yesterday than we really cared for.

I do sincerely hope your mother is well by now. She looked so tired at the hospital. I'm afraid your sister's wedding will be a little much for her.

I wonder if you have ever spoken to her about our plans for the future?

Please write me often Alice, although it may take several weeks between each time you hear from me. And remember I'll always love you dear, with all my heart. And I'll be counting the days till we meet again.

My best regards to you all.

Jens

MAIL FROM ENGLAND

Graves are supposed to be a person's final resting place, but you are restless with me at Eden Brook. I know there can be no going back to before The Jens Album. So I will write for you and live quiet for awhile.

Today you are 17 going on 21, as Uncle John would say. Studying for your exams. Jens is in England.

Spring, 1941.

Number 588 Lansdowne Avenue, Westmount, Quebec.

Alice opens the door, barely letting the hinges squeak as she edges sideways into the hallway. She closes the door slowly, holding the latch so the catch won't click.

There is no mail on the table by the door. She stands for a minute at the bottom of the stairs listening for Big Marjorie upstairs. Say Mother. Think Big Marjorie. Keep it straight.

Then she hears the sliding silk of bed covers. Then the bell's silver ring.

"Alice? Is that you?" Big Marjorie calls and shakes the bell again.

Alice leans against the door and closes her eyes. Maybe if she pretends she is not there the bell will stop.

"Alice!" The tone has changed from a question to a demand.

Alice opens her eyes. "Yes," she calls back.

"You're late. School was out an hour ago. I've been waiting for you."

"I told you I was going to be studying. Matrics start in a month. I need to study."

"Well, I needed you this afternoon. That lazy Annie has taken the day off again and I haven't had my tea."

77

"I'll make it for you and bring it up in a minute."

Alice drops her books on the stairs and goes into the kitchen. Annie has left Big Marjorie's silver inlaid teapot and matching cups on the counter. Alice fills the kettle and sets it on the stove.

There's an envelope on the table with "Alice" written on it in her father's fast scrawl. Probably an apology. She opens it.

Dear Blonde Bombshell —

Sorry we quarrelled this morning. I was worried about how hard you have been studying. I thought a weekend of golf would be good for you. John and Joan are coming with me this afternoon — we will all be home Sunday night. Little Marjorie is staying with the Fairchilds.

Take good care of your mother — her nerves are bad again. The doctor says she has to be kept quiet. Call me at the Inn if you need anything.

All my love
XXX OOO

Dad

The kettle boils and she fills the teapot. Carrying the tray, she climbs the creaking stairs. Her mother is sitting up with pillows behind her back. She lifts the silver bell from the table so Alice can set the tray down.

"You may pour," Big Marjorie says.

Alice pours, adds two lumps of sugar, and passes her mother the cup and saucer. Then she sinks into the maroon velvet armchair beside the table. Her father says the colour is too bordello. She is Mrs. Tyler. She can choose any fabric she wants from his warehouse. She chose the maroon velvet. Another argument. It is her room. She will choose what she wants. He has his own bedroom.

"Dad left me a note," Alice says, her eyes closed, her head resting back on the chair. "He's taken Joan and John golfing at the Inn for the weekend."

"At least your brother and sister didn't disappoint him. He wanted you along. He's so proud of you. He loves to show all his friends his attractive daughter."

"I told him I have to study."

"What nonsense! You'll get your Matric. It doesn't matter what your marks are."

"I need good marks to get into McGill."

Big Marjorie turns her gunner eyes on Alice. "McGill! As if that was going to do you any good. You already read too many books. What's the point of going to university if all you're going to do is read more books?"

Alice feels her jaw tightening, the way it always gets hard when she's about to argue with her parents. She remembers her father's note about keeping her mother quiet and changes the topic.

"At least you and I will have the weekend together. We can play cards if you like. And I can study in my room so I'll be close by if you need anything."

Big Marjorie frowns. "I'd be happier if you were accepting invitations on the weekends like Joan. She knows how to meet the right men. Don called today and asked if you were available for supper this Saturday at the Normandy."

"What did you tell him?"

"I told him you would call him this evening."

"Oh." Alice pauses. "He'll understand when I tell him I have to study. He knows how important my exams are. When he wrote his exams last year, he barely left his house for weeks."

"And what good did that do him? He's in officer training now."

"Yes, but he can go to university when the war is over."

"The war! Are people supposed to give up their lives just because there's a war on?"

Alice sinks deeper into the armchair, wondering how long she can avoid an argument.

"Sit up straight," Big Marjorie tells her. "I suppose you're slouching like that because you're worried about your pen pal, that Norwegian pilot. What's his name?"

"Jens, Mother. Jens Müller. You met him at the Inn. You had dinner with him three times."

"Oh, yes. Now I remember. One of Officer Malm's men. Polite enough. But I expect they'll both be killed soon. I'm surprised they've lasted this long."

"Please don't say that, Mother. It's terrible."

"It's the truth, that's all. You have to be realistic about these things. I've heard England is overrun with foreigners who have lost their own countries. I imagine there are thousands of those people lolling about in London and getting in everybody's way. They should do the right thing and be the first to get shot up by the Germans. I'm sure that's what will happen to those Norwegians."

"Mother!"

"Oh, I know you and thousands of other silly girls are writing aching heart letters to keep up their spirits. That's very noble of you, Alice, doing your part for the war effort. Goodness knows I'm doing mine—inviting all those dreadful farm boys in uniform to our dinner parties. But you mustn't think there's anything more to it than that. When the war's over, everything will go back to the way it was before. Everybody will be back in their right place. You'll see."

Alice shakes her head and is about to reply when Big Marjorie interrupts. "Oh, don't look so gloomy. You're going to have a wonderful life. Much better than mine with all my sorrows. You have everything I never had. You have a mother who loves you. And when the war is over, everything will work out for you just as I have planned. And I will have a home at the top of Westmount Boulevard."

Alice tries to smile.

"That's better," Big Marjorie says. "Now that you're smiling I have a surprise for you. You received two letters this morning. One from that Norwegian and one from the Cochonds. They want you to ride their horses in our show at the Alpine Inn this summer. Won't that be grand? And Joan will be riding our horses. I wonder who will get the most ribbons—you or her? Probably Joan. Little Marjorie and her Wilfred have promised to help me with the guests. Isn't this turning out splendidly? Don't I take the best care of my girls."

Big Marjorie slides two envelopes out from under her blanket. "Here's your letters, my dear. And please return my tray to the kitchen."

Alice sits in the kitchen. She turns over the envelope from Jens and inspects the sealed flap. Big Marjorie would open it if she could. How many letters has she intercepted? Jens has written saying she must not have received all his letters.

Yes, he is still wearing her school pin in the liner of his flying helmet. And here's a photo of him with her pin painted on his fighter plane. Beside it he

Flying With Alice. Jens piloted this Hawker Hurricane Mk II on
missions from England with Alice's school crest on the fuselage,
her pin in his helmet, and her photo in his jacket.

has stencilled ODIN. The Norse god of warfare. He flies with her photo in
his jacket.

But he never says anything about his missions. Are they dangerous? Are
many pilots missing? Presumed dead.

Everything is censored, he writes. Everything but my love for you.

But at 588 Lansdowne Avenue, Westmount, Quebec, even love is censored.

LOVE AND MORE

It is a time of great uncertainty, made worse for you and Jens by the slow and irregular delivery of mail by transatlantic ship. The Nazis have captured France. It should be a time of despair, but he writes today with an optimism that seems misplaced. "I may be with you sooner than I thought." Amazing, isn't it, that his plans are all on one goal, to return to you.

June 6, 1941

Darling!

It seems years and years ago since I was with you the last time. Though when looking at the present, time seems to fly and I may be with you sooner than I thought. I've been missing you so much Alice, and the day I may hug you again I'll be the happiest and most grateful of all. I love you Alice, as I've never loved before and never will. Your influence has wakened sleeping qualities within me it seems, qualities which I have neglected to develop in the most crucial way. But I know I'll be able to bring them up to standard level. And so I look at the future with much optimism. You bet your sweet life I'll reach our dreams and make them come true.

. . . . Jens.

P.S. Do you remember the last hours we spent together in 588, you

K27LNLD LONDON 24 27 1358 LC   *"Via Marconi"*

MISS ALICE TYLER
588 LANSDOWNEAVE MONTREAL

THANKS FOR YOU SWEET TELEGRAM AND LETTERS LOVING YOU AND MISSI
NG YOU MORE THAN EVER

JENS MULLER

MARK YOUR REPLY *"Via Marconi"* AND FILE AT ANY CANADIAN PACIFIC TELEGRAPH OFFICE
OR CALL MARQUETTE 8144

"Loving You." The Jens Album contained 99 letters and telegrams.
Alice never knew how many her mother intercepted.

were teasing me and assuring me your words would haunt me? Well,
they do. I'll love you forever darling, so very much!

September 9, 1941

Dearest,

For over one month I hadn't heard a word from you and I started
wondering what was happening. Then suddenly come eight letters
one day. It made me feel quite a new person. The way you write Alice
brings me so close to you and Canada, although it sometimes takes
me awhile to find out what you have written. I find it takes quite a lot
of practice, of which I hadn't had nearly as much as I had in Toronto,
where I, in the end, could read your letters quite fluently. But I'll stop

teasing you darling, because I love everything with you, even your handwriting, — And then I haven't such a wonderful writing myself. I know I've not at all written enough to you dearest, and the only excuse I have is that I haven't felt like writing anybody, not even you.

I must congratulate you with passing your exam, although it's rather late to do that now, but I only today received your letters telling of it. And besides with your brains it would hardly be a difficult task.

...As always, I'll be dreaming and thinking of you Alice.

Your Jens

October 8, 1941

Darling,

Some people think it not wise to tell the person one is in love with, too clearly of this love. However, I find it most wonderful to be able, without any need of hesitation, to tell you unreservedly of my love for you Alice; that I love you with all my heart, and that you can always feel sure darling, that nothing and nobody shall ever be able to change my love for you, which has, if possible, grown stronger and more sincere during the time we have been apart.

I shall close for this time. I only want to tell you once more that I love you so much Alice. So very much.

Your Jens

The Social Scene: Another of your clippings, now in Alice's Suitcase. This one features you as the clever young rider of Ste. Adele and among the prominent entrants in the coming Military Show at St. Jerome Army camp. I see you've already won ribbons in other shows. Well done. This will be a nice reminder for me that you always looked good on a horse.

October 25, 1941

Darling,

Today is quite an occasion. I think I remember correctly when saying that it is your birthday today. I wonder if you remember what you once said you wanted me to give you today?

This makes me think, however, of what I shall do for a living when this war is over. To pilot a plane is about all I have learned thoroughly, and what use have I of that with all the pilots let loose after the war? Never the less, I do my best to absorb some navigation & such, which a commercial pilot, with any self-respect, ought to know.

My highest ambition is to be able to marry you darling, and make you happy.

I hope your feelings for me will still be the same after some years, and you will still be willing to take the chance of marrying me.

I love you as always,

Jens

December 11, 1941

Dearest,

I received your so sweet letter today & as usual it made me most happy. Later today your book of poems also arrived. Thanks ever so much darling, for both. I have only up to this moment had time to read the one of the poems you like; & the last verse, if you recall is, in effect what I promised myself the moment we parted. — Ottar came in this evening & of course started teasing me when he saw the book. We see quite a lot of each other these days. — Ottar sat reading your book when he told me of how well you write Alice.

Don't you think you could possibly favour me too with the honour of reading some of what you have written. Honestly dear, why not send me some of your writings?? I asked you once to show them to me but you seemed so unwilling that I did not dare to ask once more. If I had known then that Ottar had been granted the permission, you should not have got away with it so easily. — So please Alice?! So remember this, my one and only. I love you and always shall.

Your Jens

The Social Scene: I don't like the snobby tone of this clipping, but I'm keeping it in Alice's Suitcase. I think it is important for me to see you and your friends finding new ways to be silly and trivial and popular during the war. There you are with five other marriage prospects at a raffle for a silver fox cape donated by Holt Renfrew with proceeds going to the Queen's Canadian Fund. I despair to think this was the best you could do with your talents.

COMPLICATIONS AND COINCIDENCES

I have told nobody but Judy about my visits here. She needs to understand my galloping around in lives that took place long before I was born. I tell her My Goodbye Mother memories of 13 years have broken down the corral rails and there are horses running loose everywhere. I am a group of one gathering a scattered herd. And I'm not asking for help.

What's new? she answers.

I have brought a few letters to read with you, but first I'm going to spread out a blanket. I will be here a few hours and I may as well be comfortable. The low sun drips purple over the cloudless Rockies. I expected to see more grave visitors on a cheerful day like this. Perhaps they'll drive out after supper. By the way, the grounds crew mowed the grass this morning. Everything is neat and tidy. I suppose they drive right over top of you.

I'll start with Pilot Officer Ottar Malm's letter. You have to admire the Norwegian education system that taught English to these airmen. They write well.

May 27, 1942

Dear Alice,

Thank you very much for your letter. I can assure you that I like to hear from you very much and it is very nice of you to write and tell me all the news about the family and yourself. It sure seems a long time since we saw each other; but one day the whole thing will be over and we shall again have some fun together.

We are kept quite busy these days in Fighter Command and I have had several trips over the channel which is exciting every time.

Otherwise life goes on as usual over here. I have been here (London) 10 months now and I am getting used to the blackout and all other things that goes together with a country at war. I am looking forward very much to the time when lights again will shine in all the cities and villages of Europe and that is going to be some day!!

I find it difficult to write letters these days, everything is censored and all the things that happen around can not be known till after the war! That is of course understandable and I guess there is nothing one can do about that.

All the best to you Alice and please write again.

Love Ottar

Now here's one from Jens glued beside the picture of him with your school crest painted on his fighter named *Odin*. He always flies with your school pin in his helmet and your picture in his flight jacket.

June 6, 1942

Dearest,

The rate at which your letter parcels keep coming in is overwhelming. Some days ago I got "Life" "Reader's Digest," then the "Navigation Notebook" came the same day as two of your letters. The result is that I feel very much on top of the world. More so than I have for a long time.

I miss you very much Alice, therefore I enjoy so to hear from you; you get so near then, I can almost hear you telling me of all the things you write about.

I am sorry to hear that you have been ill again, Alice, I think your suggestion of going to school this summer to learn French or dramatics, is not a very good one. Why not take it easy with the studying for a while, rather climb Mount Baldy a couple of times a day?

Think of all the things we are going to do together when I get over to you again for good.

I love you Alice

Jens

You don't have time to answer this letter right away because you're studying for your Matrics. Bert and Big Marjorie are concerned about how hard you are pushing yourself. They don't understand that McGill is your chance to have a life of your own, away from Big Marjorie's debutante parties, coming out parties, and dinner parties. At McGill, things will be different. You'll still have to live at home, but...things will be different. You'll have your independence. Isn't that what you wanted?

This letter from your father expresses his concern for you in such a cheerful way that I think it must have been hard for you to keep your engagement from him.

Undated

To my very sweet little "Blondie,"

Your teacher Miss Nichol called Mother saying that she thought you were worrying too much about your Matric or "something" and that it was affecting your studies. Now my dear don't be silly and ruin your health. If you do not pass the world will still go on and does not matter much. Please talk to me about it because your health is more important to us than hundreds of Matrics. If you are worrying about anything else let your Dad know and we will fix it up all swell.

Love,

Dad

Could that "something" be Jens?

On June 19 you finished your Matrics and, instead of writing Jens, you sent him a telegram. Here it is: the rectangle of date-stamped, blue and red

Marconi Telegram paper that the messenger delivered to Jens's 331 Squadron Barrack.

```
PLT JENS MULLER RNAF LONDON
DEAREST HAVE JUST FINISHED MY EXAMS
LOVE YOU MORE THAN EVER
WILL WRITE SOON YOU TOO
ALICE TYLER
```

I found this telegram in your Jens Album, which didn't make sense. If you sent it to England, why was it returned to you? It took me a long time to figure that out. We'll get to the unravelling soon.

Were you disappointed when Jens didn't reply to your "Love you more than ever"?

Twelve days later you wrote Jens again.

June 30, 1942

Dearest,

Mother and John and I came over to the Inn for dinner this evening and at this point Mother is chatting with some friends so I decided to write you while I was waiting but I think we shall be leaving soon and I will finish this letter when I go home.

Well Mother and I have been sitting for two hours discussing past, future, and present and now Marjorie and she are playing cards. John keeps asking "quiz" questions and so I shall have to stop writing for awhile once more.

…Do remember me to Ottar and tell him I will write soon. As always I love you with all my heart and it doesn't matter when you come back darling because I shall still love you just as much as ever one hundred years from now—only the sooner you come back the happier I will be.

And so for now I remain
Yours as ever,

Alice

You pasted this returned to you letter in The Jens Album beside the returned telegram of June 19. Why didn't Jens keep them?

The next letter you pasted in The Jens Album came from Ottar Malm, dated June 20, 1942. Jens left for England a year ago.

"I AM VERY MUCH AFRAID"

588 Lansdowne Avenue, Westmount, Quebec

A letter today? Maybe, you think as you open the front door. Jens can be confusing. Sometimes you get two letters in a week. Other times, a letter every two weeks. You'd think he would have answered your telegram about finishing your Matrics. You wish you understood better what he was doing over there. Where is he flying that he can't tell you about? He shares his love not his dangers. Poker Face.

On the table is a letter from Ottar Malm. His handwriting is so clear. Definite. Purposeful. Most likely another of his everything is censored but don't worry life is wonderful letters with gallant references to adventures and signed With Love To Your Family, Ottar.

The house is quiet. You open Ottar's letter at the kitchen table.

June 20, 1942

My dear Alice,

Most of the times when I sit down to write letters to friends of mine I do it with pleasure. But this time it is different Alice. Our good friend Jens is missing from operations yesterday and I am very much afraid that we shall never see him again. We became involved in a dog fight somewhere in England and Jens failed to return.

I find it difficult to write and tell you this Alice, because I don't quite understand it myself, in fact none of us in the squadron from aircraft hands and up to the top man can believe that it is really so.

War is a cruel game Alice and it has taken many fine young men's lives. I have lost many good friends; in Norway, in Canada and here in England. The finest of them all was Jens, and I know that all his friends, and he only had friends, are behind me when I say that in him Norway lost one of its best and promising young men.

One gets to know the boys in a squadron because they are always together, in the air and on the ground; they go through the happy moments as well as the tough spots together; and the friendship that emerges from that sort of a life is something that is difficult to put on paper, one must be a member of the squadron to feel it and understand it. And all of us in our squadron who knew Jens as we did, know that he was the noblest and finest pilot and friend we could have.

And you lost something Alice! Jens was in love with you; you know it and so do I. You had once given him your School-pin. He always wore that, and on his aircraft he had copied and painted that same pin. He very often talked to me of you because I knew you so well. He had plans for the future after the war and the first was to go back to Canada and see you. He was a hard-working young man; he never had an idle moment, but was always reading and studying when off duty. And he would have succeeded in whatever field he would have chosen after the war.

Jens was straight and he was honest and I have never seen him do what you would call a wrong thing to do. As long as I have known him I have never heard anybody criticize Jens, or anybody say anything bad about him. That was impossible, and here on our Station his ground crew and everybody else refuses to think that he is really gone and is not coming back. But Alice, I am afraid it is not going to be so and it is hard for you; hard for us all.

I have never heard Jens refuse to do anybody a favour, he was always willing to help everybody and there were many who came to Jens and asked for favours and help of different kinds.

As I told you before Alice I find it hard to write about what has so suddenly happened. I wish I was with you now and we could have talked together and it would have been so much easier.

I would like you to write to me Alice and I want to help you in all the ways it is possible for me to do. If there is anything of Jens's belongings that you would like to have to keep in memory of him please write and tell me.

And so Alice I shall close this letter, my thoughts are with you and I know that you will keep the memory of Jens as all his other friends will do; the noblest and finest boy you have ever met!

Love, Ottar

YOUR PICTURE IN THE SILVER FRAME

Good morning. I couldn't leave you too long with Ottar's letter. Shot down Jens makes gravestones tremble. Could he still be alive? Will he come back for you as he promised?

It took me a long time to stop asking about the where and why of My Goodbye Mother's shot down railway station disappearance.

We are in Springbank today. You always liked the view from our house on top of the hill, so I expect you are just as much here as at Eden Brook. Through the poplars we can see what's left of the old Springbank dairies. The Hodgsons, the Longeways, the Andersons. That was fifty years ago. Only acreages now. I saw Dale Hodgson a few weeks ago and he reminded me that you were probably the first from the city to buy land at Springbank. The early 60s. Do you remember his parents, Claire and Alan? I used to wish we were like the Hodgsons, connected to a community of friends, parents, and relatives, chatting at school Christmas concerts, the curling rink, and the weddings. Claire had a little smile that made me feel she knew a secret that one day I might figure out. Alan talked arms folded about haying and cultivators and milking machines. He's no fool, you said. Don't underestimate Alan Hodgson.

I won't procrastinate anymore. I'm impatient, dying to show you what I brought today. A telegram dated July 23, 1942. The one that arrived 34 days after missing from operations. Not a word since then.

A month ago you closed The Jens Album. The last line written. Shot down fate decided. Your Jens lost. Presumed dead. Now you are opening the

Album to add four lines of life returned. A letter to follow. The pages ahead
to be filled with future changed.

July 23, 1942

Dear Alice,

I sent you a cable today young lady and I bet you were as glad to
receive it as I was to send it to you. The thing that we all hoped, but
never thought could be possible has happened. Jens is alive and he is
now a P.O.W. somewhere in Germany. It all sounds like a miracle and
as soon as the news [was] confirmed I sent you the cable.

   We have had a letter from him and in that he asks us to send him
different things of his belongings and amongst it your picture in the
silver frame. Well you know that I have returned it to you so I guess it
is up to you to forward it to him and I guess also that you are only too
glad to do that.

   The address is
   Jens Müller 2, LT 1007
   Stalag Luft 3
   Deutschland (Allemagne)

                                        Love, Ottar

I don't suppose Jens's new address had much meaning to anybody in Montreal
in 1942.

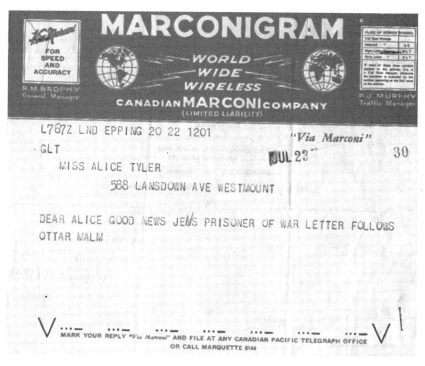

Good News. Jens's friend and fellow pilot Ottar Malm sends Alice the news that Jens is alive after being shot down over the British Channel.

SHOT DOWN

The title's a clue, isn't it? How did I find his grave? Did an ember in your handful of ashes heart just flicker into flame? Did you think I was going to make this easy? Well, you'll just have to figure it out for yourself as we go along.

Here's how Jens describes the day he was shot down. It begins with Squadrons 331 (the Norwegians), 222, and 124 taking off to patrol the Belgian and Dutch coasts. Within half an hour the pilots attack their first target: three German ships anchored in the Schelde Delta. Jens is flying a Spitfire Mk Vb equipped with four 7.7 mm Browning machine guns and two 20 mm Hispano Mk II cannons.

Then the German Focke-Wulfs arrive.

June 19, 1942. There are still no enemy planes in sight. My engine is going full bore. I look around in all directions, mostly to the rear, from where attacks usually come. There! Right under me to the left is a Spitfire with a Focke-Wulf following it closely. Another Focke-Wulf appears! Neither of them have seen me. I see no others. Why not have a shot at one of those down there? I am at a safe distance and there ought to be quite some ammunition left.

I turn round sharply and dive on the German. The guns work fine, when suddenly I see the tracer shots.

This means that ammunition is almost used up. The guns work for a second or two, then stop one after another.

I'm unarmed and quite helpless if anyone attacks. Best to get home while there is still time.

I swing around sharply, looking around for Germans. There is one! He is a long way off—a kilometre, perhaps further—and above me. The plane is silhouetted clearly against the sky, it is making straight for me. He may not have seen me. I alter course. The German also changes course. He has spotted me.

I gave full throttle long ago and now only hope the motor will hold. I climb into some thin clouds, behind which I hope to hide. The clouds are too thin, more transparent than I thought.

The German is much closer. Every time I head into a bit of cloud the German comes out of the last one. Confound it! There is another German! And yet another! The first fellow must have used his radio.

Now they open fire, their shots go past to one side of my plane. I had been expecting this for some minutes. I make a short sharp turn to get out of range of their fire, and succeed. I continue turning. It is now useless to fly straight ahead, and the twist and turns slow me down a lot.

A few minutes later the Focke-Wulfs are so close that I have to make violent turns and manoeuvres to stay out of their fire. They are now close on my tail. All I can do is dodge and that I do so the sweat pours. The Germans use a lot of tracer ammunition. It is easy to see the smoke trails in the sunlight, and easy to dodge them.

Two other Germans join the party. Now there are five of them on my tail. It is only a question of time and I am done for. A couple of sharp reports right at the back of my backrest confirm this thought. The smell of gunpowder stings my nose. Then there is a loud explosion in my engine. A shell! The Rolls (engine) starts coughing, slows down, loses power, dies out.

I cannot realize that this must be the end of my journey. I still hear my friends talking over the wireless.

A couple of shots more bring me to. I dodge, pull the nose of the plane up in order to slow down a bit. I turn the plane on to its back while I undo the safety straps and telephone wires. Then open the hood of the cockpit (the bottom is up). I push the stick forward and am thrown out of the plane.

CRAZINESS

I loved your Canmore craziness. The way you tied our toboggan behind the station wagon and tore through the snow, wheels spinning, spraying blinding banks of ice storms until we tumbled off, rolling and wondering if dead was cold.

Fingers frozen. Eyes blinking ice. Teddy finds me. The station wagon circling over the miners' golf course to pick us up. Toques slapped on our legs to break the packed snow. You righted the toboggan and away we went again.

You were fearless for us. You cracked the long whip, accelerating us on the circumference of a sliding circle. The tow rope thrumming sideways through the wake. We bounced over ruts and into the air, leaning into the centre, fingers wrapped in the toboggan's ropes. Teddy shouting to hang on. And we crashed.

I suppose you saw the empty toboggan and laughed.

What lovely craziness. Without you I'd never have gone so fast so far.

And when we were older, we had skis and tracked one behind the other on the same rope, arguing over who went in the front. We skied over top of whoever fell, not wanting to let go. What horrible tangled heaps of calling each other assholes. Do you remember the old bear trap bindings? Skis broke or legs broke. And we begged for speed and you floored that 1950s wood-panelled station wagon. Mitts frozen to the rope, we went again. Geoffrey in the back window cheering the falls. And him riding on the roof when we cruised back to the cabin.

He would be the family daredevil. The downhill skier who didn't give a

The Explorers. Alice led never turn back hiking and riding expeditions to the high meadows of the Rockies where the wild storms and long trails challenged her. (L to R) Hilda Anderson, Tyler, Teddy, Dr. Jim Anderson, Mary Anderson, and Alice.

fuck about crashing. You taught him that language and that fearlessness. God how you loved him. He'd try anything. If I said no, he said yes. He'd do it. And what an unrelenting physical genius he was. Like you. And he battled you at everything.

We take the horses for a gallop, jumping every log and brush pile we see. Geoff, me, Teddy, and you. We look back. Geoff's off. You're with him. I don't know if there's been an accident or another argument. What happened? Geoffrey fell and the horse stepped on his hand. It looks to us like his thumb is cut off. Blood everywhere. Get back on you tell him. No. He's walking. Too far, get on. No. You grab the little bastard by the back of his shirt and throw him on. He's hunched up in the saddle, barely moving. His mouth set hard, like yours. Lips tight. You get on behind and are galloping home. Trixie shies and you both fall, breaking his collarbone. Back on. He's not hurt as much as pissed off.

Over to Dr. Anderson's for stitches. A weekend and he's had a few drinks. No matter, he'll stitch him up. You lay him in the back of the station wagon.

He remembers your calm hardness. The unflinching set of your jaw. No excitement. Just determination. Don't fight me now Geoffrey. The hospital is closed. You and Dr. Anderson break a window and find the medical supplies. No anaesthetic. You hold his hand down while Dr. Anderson stitches. Geoff was the only one as tough as you. He's still mad a week later when we ride out from the cabin to camp at Spray Lakes. He has to stay home. He may never forgive us.

And when Ruthie Anderson came running. Geoff's in the bottom of the pool. And Daddy running across the grass kicking off his sneakers and diving in and pulling him out. Laid him on the bricks and pumped the water out.

Geoff was coughing water mad. I can swim. And you walk up and say no you can't. But tomorrow you will learn.

The Canmore cabin pool is murky green Bow River water freezing cold and in you throw him. The deep end. Swim. He paddles wild eyed for the side. You push him off. Swim. One length. And he's yelling all your swears back at you and you're pushing him from the edge. Swim with your mouth shut. It's easier. He makes the shallow end and you haul him out by his arm. You did it. You can swim.

He yells his fuck words and you offer him another swim. He runs off and you spend the rest of your life chasing him down.

What a great one arm twist you had. Even Teddy got the one arm march. One twist and we were obedient. Not Geoff. He stood and called you a sonofabitch. With one hand on his arm you kicked his ass lifting both his feet from the ground. Who's the sonofabitch? You are. Kick. Who's the sonofabitch? You are. Kick. It was great seeing him bounce with each kick. We cheered for both of you. He was flying. Mother of five and you kicked like one of us. You owned the yard.

Even my teenage friends were afraid of your one arm twist. I remember you marching Doug out of the Banff dance hall. Home by midnight we had promised. And in you came at 12:30 and caught him on the dance floor. He was home by 12:45. I saw his picture in the business section last year. He tracks down business crooks and marches them off to jail. I thought of phoning him and asking if he uses the arm twist you taught him.

That's the crazy you were. Don't sneak. Don't whine when things don't work out. Get back on the horse. Go again. You want to have fun in life, or do you want to whine about it. Whiners. Boy, you despised whiners. Maybe that's why you always forgave Geoff's transgressions.

Do you want another ride on the toboggan or are you going to whine? If you are, you're going home. Another ride. Who was as tough or as crazy as you?

And then one day you're sick. Or drunk. And nobody is getting their ass kicked across the yard. Nobody is learning how much fun it is to be brave and cold and sore and have their thumb almost cut off and here's a broken collarbone too. Nobody is learning to see you die. It took you years to die a second time and you didn't bitch about it.

You told me you wake up with pain and that's how it's going to be all day. You had a real fuck you attitude toward cancer.

THE LUFTWAFFE PILOTS

In the 34 days between when Jens parachuted from his Spitfire and when Ottar telegrammed to say he was in a POW camp—while you were arguing with your parents to allow you to attend McGill—here's what happened:

After parachuting from his Spitfire Jens paddled his dinghy for three days toward England—a coincidence with Santiago's three days. The current was too strong and Jens washed ashore on the Belgian coast where a German patrol captured him. The patrol marched him to their guardhouse where he was interrogated but refused to give anything but "Name, Nationality, Number, Force."

During the night, two girls cleaned his uniform and hid a Catholic medallion in his pocket—not knowing he was an atheist. The next day he was transported to Durchgangslager der Luftwaffe, a temporary camp at Frankfurt for captured airmen. Along the way to this camp, Poker Face Jens Müller had some fun when his guard stopped for a meal in a Luftwaffe pilot mess hall. Here's how Jens remembers it:

> While we sat there asking about each other's equipment, planes were taking off and landing, all Focke-Wulfs 190. It looked as though this type of plane was difficult to land, as most of them swerved to one side on landing, which could also mean that German airmen were not well trained. Four machines were parked 25 metres from our table, but I got no chance to have a look at them. At last I asked outright if I could

look into one of the cockpits. They laughed heartily at this, as I had expected them to.

Later they told me one thing before we left was that some days ago they had shot down two Spitfires at the mouth of the Schelde. This gave me food for thought.

KRIEGSGEFANGENENPOST

After another interrogation, the Germans released Jens into Dulag Luft I near Frankfurt where he was allowed to send a letter to you.

Like all his letters after his capture it was written on official folded twice Kriegsgefangenenpost letter forms read and stamped by the Nazi censors. Then by Allied censors. Maybe by Big Marjorie. Crumbly dry now pasted in your Jens Album.

June 26, 1942

Dearest,

Things have been happening rather quickly lately, & I have ended up in a situation which isn't exactly to my taste. However so far everything is all right. I had to bale out, & I was taken prisoner. I'll tell you about it when we meet again. I only hope you haven't received too bad news about me dear, & that you haven't worried, because I suppose Ottar has told you I was missing. The treatment we get is O.K. But I would appreciate if you would send me some food, & if you do don't forget the peanut butter! How about some thick stockings for the winter, & the pullover you promised me?!

Thank heavens I always brought one of the photos I took of you at the hill just behind your house up north. It is somewhat worn by seawater, because I spent three days in the dinghy, but I can tell you that I treasure it. As always Alice I love you with all my heart, & shall forever. And please write often Dearest.

Your Jens

106

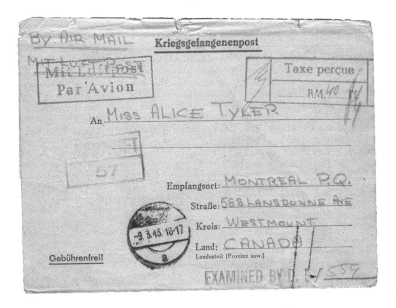

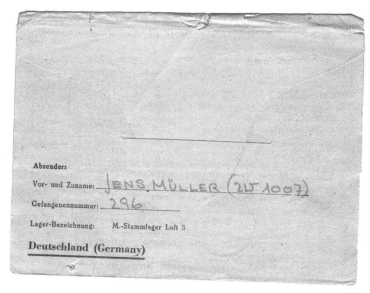

Kriegsgefangenenpost from Stammlager Luft III. Jens never hinted to Alice about the escape plans in his letters, only repeating his promise to return for her…and that he would always love her.

Typical Jens, isn't it? He loves you with all his heart. He hopes his misfortune didn't cause you to worry. The best line, of course, is about your photo "somewhat worn by seawater." I expect some German collected your pin from his helmet.

Jens would be kept at Dulag Luft I in Germany for almost two weeks before being transported by train to Stalag Luft III in Poland. There is so much of him in this letter. He's not concerned about himself… "it is quite an interesting experience," but he's worried about the money you'll need to buy him books and food (as if you were broke!). All he wants from you is a photo. How many men did you know like that?

July 5, 1942

Dearest,

I am now at a permanent camp & longing very much to hear from you, & when you write, please send photos of you all! I am in a room with four Canadians one from N.Z. & one from England. Very nice fellows too. However I know better things to do the rest of the time this war will last, although it is quite an interesting experience.

There is lots of time in which to read & study as you can imagine, & the library here is not too bad. I am afraid I shall have to ask you to do some work for me again. If you find it possible please send me food-parcels through the Red Cross. Here they say the best way is to send through the American Red Cross. Parcel no. 6. Any kind of food.

You see, I want to do a lot of reading. I hope you received the 10£ I sent you for the books, Alice. I shall write my unit & ask them to send you the necessary funds for the parcels, if you will be so kind & send them as often as possible. Well darling this wasn't much of a letter I am afraid, & I promise the next ones shall have different contents. I love you more than ever Alice & I am thinking of you so much. My best to all of you, & don't forget the photos! With all my love I remain,

Your Jens

P.S. Peanut butter.
P.S. Please acknowledge my letters.

THE TIVOLI

My heart trembled for you My Goodbye Mum when I read Jens's first letter from Stalag Luft III. I know now but of course you and Jens couldn't know what was coming. Dare to escape! The Geneva Convention — 50 prisoner executions... Of course Jens would try. He has promised to return for you.

I wish I could have warned you. You had already lost then found Jens when he was shot down, now I am sure you will lose him forever at Stalag Luft III. The German high-security camp; 10,000 restless airmen inside barbed wire and gun towers.

The Great Escape starring Steve McQueen opens in 1963 at Calgary's Tivoli Theatre. Grade Ten Jim phones want to go?

You drop us off at the door. Not a reveal. We pay. The film starts. He rattles Maltesers from his box. Inspecting them one at a time before pushing them one at a time between his lips. Lingering. Glancing up between wiping chocolate smears on his pants.

Suddenly I recognize this. The marching. The orders. The barracks. Boarding school. Stalag Luft III. I slouch down and stare cold at the familiarity of lives controlled.

I am a Prisoner of War. The moonless night of March 24, 1944. A tunnel named Harry: 30 feet deep and 330 feet long. Disguised. Forged papers. Go! Sand dripping onto my head through that shoulder-wide claustrophobic tunnel 30 feet below the wire. Climbing the ladder and seeing black trees 10 feet away. The guard box 90 feet away. The tug on the signal rope. I dash across wet snow. Some racing to railway stations. To freight yards. I imagine freedom.

The patrol is stopping me by the road. Here are my travel documents. A German pistol cold caresses my neck. Only three got away.

Jim buys another box of Maltesers as we leave and eats them one at a time as we wait for you. He talks on and on about Steve McQueen's motorcycle ride.

I am shot in the back of the head and wordless spinning down into the fear of surviving two more years of school.

See you next term Jim is all I can say.

The Great Escape was the last film I saw at the Tivoli. I hated the theatre and I hated Maltesers. They were the seeing and the not knowing.

Somewhere in all our years I mentioned the film. You said you were in love with one of the pilots. You were drinking and I wasn't paying attention.

I don't know if I can read more letters from the Album knowing how this is going to end for you and Jens. "We regret to inform you..."

CHRISTMAS EVE

You were the most glimmering woman in every house we visited on Christmas Eve.

We dressed in white shirts, long pants with nothing allowed in the pockets, and I couldn't wear my turquoise beaded belt. Lace-up polished shoes. Daddy splashed Vitalis Oil into his hands, smacked them together and rubbed our hair to make it shine. Then he held our chins and parted our hair with his brush, dragging the wiry bristles over our scalps. It was as if he thought our hair was fighting back, resisting him. I was glad I wasn't his horse.

We sat on the edge of the living room chairs being good while you dressed and Daddy warmed up his black going to the office car. We could hear the taps running and the toilet flushing. Geoffrey itched to start something but didn't dare.

We waited. What's she doing we whispered. You spun out of the dark hall into the light. Shiny and swirly. An electric comet on high heels. A drink in one hand, a du Maurier in the other. It was Christmas. We were celebrating.

Daddy had his arm around your waist and you stretched up to kiss his cheek. He turned and kissed your lips. My best focused picture of my Mummy and Daddy. His Vitalis hair brushed straight back.

You in the car with baby Randolph in your arms his one-year-old smile permanently on. I sat by the window behind you. I watched your long hair sifting over the top of the seat as you wrapped your fur collar over your shoulders. Daddy turned and warned us. Sit still. Be quiet. No roughhousing. The roads are bad. He has chains and shovels and flares and green army boxes labelled emergency rations in the trunk. You are talking to Daddy who drives slowly along Elbow Drive. I don't like these icy roads he says. That's because you're British you say. They are nothing to worry about. We drove all winter on roads like this in Montreal. I'll drive.

Be serious, Alice.

Your hand reaches between the door and the seat and secretly tugs my leg. I love you too.

The first visit was always business. Best behaviour. Teddy carrying blankets with Randolph inside. Ring the doorbell. Shake hands. People Daddy works with. Two barking grey Scottie dogs instead of kids. You may sit here. Would you like a slice of cheese? My legs swing back and forth under the chair. Can't touch anything. Fragile breakable don't touch everywhere. Gold rimmed plates and cups balanced on tippy tables with white frilly doilies. Doilies. What a word. Scottie dogs glaring at me. A glass of ginger ale? No thank you. Daddy glaring at my legs.

More sherry? You are in a tall chair one leg crossed over your knee. Glass balanced. Your leg swings. I look into your blue eyes and you wink. Bored. The old lady passing around a gold edged plate with shiny white glazed slices of Christmas cake. A little plate for everyone. A little napkin for everyone. A little slice for everyone. Very nice Daddy tells her. Not dry at all. A Scottie jumps on the footstool and barks at my little slice. How cute. He wants some too the old man giggles. Here you go. No! The old lady shakes her finger at me.

Randolph stinks. Can't you smell him? He's squirming. Teddy is such a good boy changing him. Thank you Teddy. Yes, we should be going. Thank you. Shake hands. I slide across the ice to the car. First there. Let's go. Teddy's not enjoying his responsibilities. But he's learning.

The Kellys will be waiting for us. This is going to be fun. We're staying behind you but almost running on the driveway so you can ring the bell and give Mr. Howard Kelly a kiss. In your glimmering swirling shining you are an announcement. You have arrived. Come in Mr. Howard Kelly deep voiced lawyer walks you through the door ignoring us.

Leona Kelly. She likes kids. Shakes our hands in age order. Teddy. Me. She smiles as she shakes my hand. Young man she calls me. Geoffrey, Billy, and Randolph stinky again. What's he been eating? Geoffrey holds his nose and blows a fart through his lips. Daddy slaps his hand.

We bump in the hall taking off our coats and then Leona has presents with our names on them. We can open them now and everybody has something to play with. We're supposed to call her Mrs. Kelly but what a summer flower sound Leona is and she gives us a hug whenever she feels like it. I get hugged by everything good.

Downstairs. The best basement I've ever been in. Linoleum. Big leather chairs. No adults down here. Come up Leona calls and have something to eat if you want.

And on the wall Indian paintings. Not postcards from Banff. Real Indians. Indians on horses. Indians with feathers. Indians with big noses. Indians staring at me. People Indians. And real Indian bows and lances and shields. Geoffrey wants to take one down and try it.

They are just standing around having drinks upstairs. Why don't they come down here and look at this stuff? Can I freshen that up for you? That's what adults say.

We're going now. A last look at the Indians. Get your coat on. Dad's pushy. Always ordering us around. Sit here. Be quiet. Back in the car. The Kellys have Indian paintings downstairs I tell you. Indians! I bet you'd like to be one you say. Like my grandmother Eva. It slips vodka out and nobody notices. Except wondering me.

We're going to the Strachan's for Christmas Dinner. They live in a summer leaf green England house with a veranda on a hill. Uncle Mike is our doctor. He brings his stethoscope when we are sick and looks very serious as he tells you Billy's stomach ache is munkhouser disease. He makes you laugh. Munchausen I figure out later. He's an everything possible person. He knows slender finger magic with coins and what makes music. He takes your pulse and barely touches you.

June has a green velvet dress this year that Daddy says is very nice. She rides horses and has pictures of red jacket foxriders jumping over hedges on the walls and placemats with long-legged horses arching their necks with villages far in the background. She's got everything planned. Christmas crackers with toys and Chinese fortunes and paper hats that don't fit sliding over our eyes.

Uncle Mike operates on his patient every year, sharpening the biggest scalpel in the kitchen drawer to amputate a leg. He always wears his paper Christmas hat and sometimes his glasses don't sit right and he bumps them back with his wrist waving the scalpel around the table taking orders for body parts.

And everybody is laughing at Uncle Mike's operations and June is calling it nonsense and can't help laughing too and lucky Susan and Charlie cheer Uncle Mike their father. He plays the piano with taking your pulse careful hands after we eat. Nobody in our family can sing but the Strachans can. There are drinks and wine and desserts on fire and sherry and du Mauriers for you dazzling the night with your Venezuelan adventures. And later there is something for the road.

We drive through Mount Royal looking at decorations and Daddy says we can drive to the Country Club and see the lights. On the way home it is snowing and I'm beside the dark window.

Your mother's had too much to drink he says. I scratch a hole in the frost and watch the snowflakes swoop by. I reach between the seat and door and let my hand tell you I am there.

The next morning is Christmas and Santa's writing is just like yours so he must have woken you up to fill the stockings. I am very funny you say squeezing me hard against you until I am quiet. Geoff and I get skis with steel edges and boots and poles and we ski in our pyjamas on the living room carpet. After pancakes and bacon and the boys have done the dishes for Mum who is tired we're going to the cabin at Canmore for the rest of the holidays and skiing at Sunshine and Norquay and Temple. Thank you Mum these are just what I wanted. Exactly like the ones we looked at in the store.

And because it is Christmas you and Daddy have a short one. Then freshen it up. Because it is Christmas morning and you're feeling better.

SECRET LIVES

You are now at McGill, supposedly looking for a husband. Jens is in Stalag Luft III, supposedly biding his time until the war is over. In fact, he is becoming part of the best organized prisoner escape of the war, and the one that ended most tragically.

A year to plan and dig 30 feet down, shoulder wide, 330 feet long, to free 200 airmen March 24/25 from a camp designed to be escape-proof. Big X: the Mastermind is Squadron Leader Roger Bushell RAF. Executed March 29, 1944.

Escape tunnels are a secret story within a secret life within a POW camp. Don't know — can't tell. Hide it from the goons. Hide it from each other. Keep the secret close. Only a few exceptional unflinching men can hide their thoughts. Poker faces. Blackmailers and forgers. Arm twisters. Tested men good with their hands. Minds that can see tools inside scraps of metal. Quick-witted men who can answer back in guttural German. We need you, Jens. But not a word to anybody. Not even that somebody of love letters. Say or write tunnel and we all die. We need men who can plan. We need men who have a purpose. We need you Jens. You have someone to escape to. She is waiting for you.

They whisper. The tunnel needs air. Can you build a bellows? Can you deliver air to men digging 30 feet below? Not a hint to anybody. Not a word to her. Not a whisper of hope until the war is over.

You, too, are a prisoner. Jens's letters reveal love but conceal escape. Not a word. You conceal secret love between the McGill library stacks. Always reading. Trust no one with the secret. Term papers. Exams. Not a word about your love. Trapped in Big Marjorie's internment camp of debutante balls and dinner dances. Meet Panzer-eyed Mother Commandant at the dinner table. Be poker-faced. Oh yes, Don is handsome. Give me time. Eligible and with prospects. A good Westmount family. Perhaps. Give me time. I have to study now.

Not a word to your best friend Betty. Not a smile to your father. Not a hint to your brother.

The Social Scene: This clipping features a photo of you, Miss Alice Tyler, in charge of the program for *Modes for Morale* being held at the Mount Royal Hotel. The proceeds of this doing your part evening will help provide entertainment for the troops. (And a night of fine dining for Montrealers. I bet the old boys loved you.)

You play your game of hidden heart. Flirt and fade. Postpone. Delay. Look the other way. Never commit. Wait for Jens. Wait.

September 25, 1942

Dear Alice,

Thank you very much for your last letters, it is good to hear from you! It certainly was a surprise to hear that Jens had been so long in a dinghy, he must have had a hell of a journey I gather. I haven't heard anything from my brother Erik yet, but I am not giving up hope that he is all right and I shall still wait some time before I take steps to inform the family at home. I hope and think that Jens will be off all right as far as food and clothing is concerned. I have spoken to the Norwegian Red Cross and they send him parcels regularly every week and that, together with parcels from his friends should prove to be ample enough for living.

All the best!

Love, Ottar

Ottar does not know that brother Erik has been dead for two months, shot down over France, July 24, 1942. His hope does not change the truth.

The Royal Norwegian Consulate General delivers a brown envelope to 588 Lansdowne Avenue, sealed with red wax.

> Dear Miss Tyler: — I am returning three letters and one cable
> addressed to 2 Ltn. Jens Müller and regret to inform you that 2 Ltn.
> Jens Müller is a prisoner of war in Germany.
>
> Yours sincerely
>
> Officer in Charge of Personnel

The brown envelope explains your returned telegram and letter in The Jens Album. I wonder what happened to the other two letters the consulate returned. Big Marjorie?

I HAVE GREAT FAITH IN OUR FUTURE

By the end of 1942, five months after Jens was locked into Stalag Luft III, you have written him 20 letters, almost 1 a week. He has written you only 3. This one probably arrived just before Christmas. It has the British tone of his mostly RAF fellow POWs and a little practical reflecting.

November 20, 1942

Dearest Alice,

It is a long time since I wrote you the last time, but there are so many to write to that it is difficult to make the allowed amount of letters do. — At this date I have received 20 letters from you since I became "un-stuck."

Your picture arrived, as did a parcel of chocolate. Thanks very much Alice. You see at this place chocolate is the camp's gold standard so to speak, because a bar costing 15¢ in Canada, POWs pay $25 for among themselves. So if you can send chocolate, sweets or anything eatable it will be most appreciated & welcome.

However, I know very well how difficult it must be for you in Canada to imagine the life of POW — With regards to books I trust your good taste & common sense so much in that direction that I am sure any book you find is good reading, will be worthwhile for me to read also. The trouble is that by the time I send a letter to you asking for a particular book, & till I receive it almost one year may elapse. — However, I suppose you know all this already so I'll leave this boring subject. — As always Alice to hear from you brings back the memories vividly, although they always are clear in my mind. I have responded to your good advice & have started learning French. Although this language was quite an important subject the last two years of school in Norway, I was even more lazy then & didn't absorb anything after the syllabus, so here I have to start from scratch.

By now I have received a number of letters from my Mother & Brother, who are O.K., which is most encouraging, especially when I have not heard from them since Xmas 1940.

I have great faith in our future Alice, but it is sure it will take a lot of sacrifice & halfway meeting on both parts at start. Most certainly our life together will be very delightful & exciting, but I do not think for a moment it will resemble the time we spent together. You know very well what I have to my credit both materially & spiritually. I hope you will show the necessary patience with me, & realize how different we are in many ways our lives have been different, our thoughts, habits, customs, views, ambitions etc. all differ considerably. (Quite good, eh?)

Well Alice, for this time so long. My best to you all, & all my love to you dearest.

                                                    Jens

P.S. PLEASE SEND BY AIRMAIL.

DONNY

Why doesn't Jens write more often?

You ask Ottar. He replies:

January 10, 1943

Dear Alice,

Thank you very much for your last letter. I am sorry that I haven't written you before, but that is partly due to circumstances that Joan could tell you. I wrote and told her about an adventure I had in the middle of last month where I was lucky enough to escape.

You must not be impatient if you do not hear from Jens as often as you would like to, but the thing is that he is only allowed to send a very limited number of letters and cards each month. I got a card from him at Christmas and he is in good spirits. He has company from another Norwegian fellow now, a very nice boy that we lost during Dieppe in August. I only hope that the year of 1943 will bring Jens back to us again.

Love, Ottar

Knowing how difficult it is for Jens to write doesn't make the waiting easier. How long can the war last?

Then Big Marjorie corners you. You are caught. Trapped. Committed. Engaged to Don! Postpone. Argue. Fight. You cannot tell Jens. Your friend Shirley writes in mid-March 1943:

Saturday Night

Dear Alice,

I have been hearing reports on you from all kinds of sources and finally decide that what I heard must be true and so I'm writing to tell you how wonderful I think it is that you're engaged!

Donny always seemed like such a sweet and nice boy whenever I've seen him—I know that sounds soupy but I mean it! I want to wish you every happiness and I'm sure that you'll have it.

I suppose that of course it will mean the end of college for you but don't let us lose touch with each other! At least you won't have Zoology to worry about.

...Lots of love and best of luck

Shirley

I suppose that means the end of college for you? Why?

Can you escape? Write Jens. Send parcels. Knit socks. Trust him to trust you.

The hidden heart breaks to read his Kriegsgefangenenpost letters. Censored. Intercepted. Read by guards to their girlfriends. Read by Big Marjorie? Always a single page folded twice. Neatly written. Each word of love considered. Measured.

How can you tell him of your prison? How unbearable is your Westmount Members Only compound compared to German machine guns and dogs? You say nothing.

Maybe you are just a pretty debutante with a wealthy family. Maybe you are wrong to want a life of your own. Who can you turn to?

Every day you are beaten down a little more by Big Marjorie. She's too powerful. Too experienced. Too determined. Too enduring.

Jens's letters of never mentioned escape and yours of never said matrimonial ambush criss-cross the Atlantic heavy with questions unanswerable.

Barbed wire and social etiquette are no response to love.

"ONE DAY NEARER THE DAY OF PEACE"

February 28, 1943

Dear, Dear Alice,

To give you a receipt of all the letters you have sent me since
I last wrote you would fill this letter. In addition, one cigarette parcel,
two book parcels containing Pocketbook editions ledgers & pencils,
& one clothing parcel, all of which arrived complete as specified in
the accompanying lists. Thanks very much all of you!! — I noticed you
had made sure the socks would fit; & they do too! — From any point
of view it must be a relief for you to start at college where you more
or less can choose the subjects that interest you. However I believe
you like & are interested in most subjects. — Here one day follows the
other without any appreciable excitements or variations. I have been
reading a lot the last months, but mostly textbooks, which makes one
feel some-what fed up after a while, especially when one realizes how
unconceivably thickskulled one has gradually become. However I have
a lot of good English & Norwegian non-educational books which
give quite a lot of relaxation. The amount of textbooks I have now
would take me years to digest, quite apart from the fact that although
I would have been able to understand them before the war, I now
find I have to revise more & more to have a hope of reading them
intelligently. I have heard from Ottar twice. They are very lazy as far

as writing is concerned in England. Well, Alice dear, we are one day nearer the day of peace!

Yours as ever, Jens

P.S. My best to you all.

Of course, no mention of his involvement in the tunnelling.

"A SMALL JOB IN THE UNDERGROUND"

I was too new in the camp to be included in any schemes. I kept myself occupied. Read a great deal, walked rounds and took part in gymnastics arranged by Englishmen. The food gradually improved. Red Cross parcels began to arrive so we were not starving. And we could go in for sport and gymnastics. When the weather was so bad that it wasn't fun to walk rounds, or when I was tired of reading, I started making things, teaspoons, bookcases and kitchen utensils. The spoons and small gadgets I made came in handy.

The fact that I could use my hands a bit helped me, without my realizing it, to a small job in the underground organization. One evening Wally came home after one of his customary absences and asked quite casually if I could make a large pair of bellows. I was sure this could be done if we could find the right materials and tools. Tools were strictly prohibited in the camp, and all sorts of materials, from nails to pieces of wood and string were very hard to get. Wally grew very thoughtful but said no more.

A couple of days later he asked me to join him after the roll call when the Germans had left. He took me to a room in one of the barracks. Several other men were there. Some were changing into old shabby clothes. We remained there some minutes. Wally was soon having an earnest conversation with one of these men. I only stood by looking at them. A certain atmosphere of excitement was in the air. The climax came when a man stuck his head in at the door and said: "All Clear."

Wally then opened the trap door to a tunnel and a few minutes later brought up a broken bellows they had been using to pump fresh air into the tunnel. Jens rebuilt and improved the bellows and was kept busy working on the camp's first tunnels, ones that were always discovered by the guards. It would be a year before the prisoners were able to complete a tunnel.

Jens also met several other Norwegian airmen in the camp, including Halldor Espelid and Per Bergsland, with whom he was photographed in the camp.

Per [Bergsland] or "Pete" as he was called was the next Norwegian to arrive. He was also to be sent to Schubin, Poland. Like many other Norwegian airmen "Pete" had also flown under a false name, an English one (Rocky Rockland), for precautionary reasons. They were men who were on the German black list before escaping from Norway and were not certain the Germans would respect the Geneva Convention if they were taken prisoners.

Respect for the Geneva Convention...a subtle way of saying they were afraid the Germans would shoot prisoners attempting to escape—as prisoners were honour-bound to try—despite their agreement to the Convention.

A NASTY TRAIT

I don't have another of my stories ready for you today. I try to leave one with you every time I visit, but your engagement to Don has me confused. I can see Big Marjorie is unrelenting in wanting her own way—a nasty trait that drives away the people she loves—and you are doing your best to stand up to her demand: Get married! Too bad you don't dare tell her about Jens. Too bad Big Marjorie didn't teach you wanting is different than needing. Wanting turns everyone nasty.

AN APOLOGY

I apologize for the remark I made last visit about Big Marjorie's nastiness. I don't like the way she twists love to get what she wants—ultimately the house on top of Westmont Boulevard. But you gave in, and not telling Jens about your engagement to Don made you look opportunistic. I know you're not like Big Marjorie. Sorry.

It is now the spring of 1943. I have to tell you I'm gossipy fascinated by this situation. You're still engaged to Don. You're still enrolled at McGill. Jens is in Stalag Luft III and you have no idea he is preparing to escape.

You've finished your first year at McGill and, escaping temporarily—if that was ever possible—from Montreal and Big Marjorie, you're writing stories in your spare time at St. Marguerite's.

And waiting.

MY LOVE FOR YOU

June 24, 1943

Dearest Alice,

Today I received one of the sweetest letters you ever wrote to me. Before I write anything more I want you to know Alice, that I love you as always, & I shall return to tell you that I feel exactly the same way as I have since I met you. Dearest if I, after I was shot down & got time to think of the future, ever doubted if I should go to Canada when peace came, it was not because my love for you had faded the least, but for the reasons I so often have pointed out to you. But the time of this doubting is gone long ago, so be prepared to see me back in Montreal soon after the war. To know of your faith in me Alice, fills me with a peculiar, delightful feeling which I have never experienced before. I think I appreciate the full value of your faith in me. —Lately I have been thinking much about how to make a living. Why not sell Norwegian skis as a start, & then perhaps gradually build up a ski factory. I am sorry to say so Alice, but so far I have not seen a good Canadian-made ski. —Please learn, young lady, that in this camp it is an observed fact that almost all of the Canadians get photos in nearly every letter from home. —The 19th of June it was one year since I was shot down. Time has flown away, & soon I hope to be with you again. Please greet your family from me, & please do not read too much Alice.

Love, Jens

TRY NOT TO FORGET AN OLD FRIEND

The Social Scene: Here's a clipping that makes me imagine Big Marjorie has ensured her number one asset is in the spotlight. It features you, Miss Alice Tyler, wearing a natural lynx coat over a honey beige corduroy suit, at the Holt Renfrew Fashion Show held, of course, at the Alpine Inn for the benefit of the Canadian Red Cross.
You look gorgeous.

The next letter is the last of many from Don. Too bad he couldn't have known about Jens instead of breaking his heart over you. Uncle John told me you ended your engagement to Don by throwing his ring across the room at a party (very big) and shouting, "I'll never marry you." Don, as the Tyler family often reminded you later, went on to do very well. (Palms down.)

July 18, 1943

Dear Alice,

I was up in the park tonight sitting all by myself thinking of the times I had been there with you and wishing you were there now, but knowing that you were having quite a time where you are.

I have been coming home for the last week twice a day and have been left disappointed twice a day.

I realise that I don't mean anything any more but surely you could take time out to give a moment to an old friend who does care and I'm afraid always will.

...Well Alice try not to forget an old friend to whom you mean so much and remain your same sweet self.

Loads of love,

Don

The Social Scene: In the Alice's Suitcase medley of arranged love, irony, honesty, and idiosyncrasies I keep your this tells it all clipping from an Alpine Inn Horse Show, just as Uncle John described it. Very Big. Check out the show-off crowd:

Mrs. W.R.G. Holt and her son are being photographed as they arrive in an old-fashioned horse-drawn brougham. Extremely classy (i.e., expensive). She's the daughter of wealthy industrialist Herbert Holt, reported to be the richest man in Montreal. Her son had better stay clear of Panzer Eyes. And over by the announcer are Sir Frederick and Lady Bowhill—he's the influential leader of the RAF Ferry Command that is sending new fighter planes overseas. I hope you flashed your blues and told him he'd better send a rescue mission to Stalag Luft III—special delivery! And in the stands is young Louis Valois who should be paying more attention to the horses than to the blonde Alice Tyler sitting beside him.

NO SIGN OF LIFE

Jens writes again, reassured. His letter is dated November 14, almost a month after you sent the one he refers to. It must have been difficult for both of you to keep hope alive when even a simple question in a letter might take two months to be answered.

November 14, 1943

Dearest,

Your letter dated Sept. 26th-43 was waiting for me on the table when I came back from the library for lunch, & I was delighted, to say the least, with hearing from you again Alice, especially after such a long time with no sign of life from you.

On Sundays I usually let the studies rest, & write letters or read fiction instead. In order to get something done during the weekdays, I have also found it necessary to work out a routine & follow that as closely as possible. — The news from home [is] good as usual; my mother & brother write very often. Ottar & friends in England have been very lazy. I hope to hear from you soon again Dearest.

Love to you all!

Your Jens

A hint?... "In order to get something done during the weekdays." What is the "something" he has to get done during the weekdays?

BYRON AND SHELLEY

I find some insight into how you are spending your away from Big Marjorie time in this letter from an admirer, Bill, stationed in Quebec.

My Dear Alice,

You know, it's a dreamlike opportunity you have up there, in your fastness of St. Marguerites, for literary inspiration. Afternoons of skiing etc. (Mornings for sleep of course) and then devote those soft, moonlit hours of mystery in the evening, to reading and writing.

Personally, I should commandeer a dormered upper room entirely for my own cultural nocturnes.

Byron and Shelley beneath the stars!

The magic of Brahms amidst moonbeams, dusting the soul of tranquillity! Ah!

Well, Alice old girl, I eagerly await a line from you—and more promptly than mine.

Sincerely, Bill

The life you wanted was so close. Writing stories at St. Marguerite's away from Big Marjorie while you wait for Jens's release. He, along with the other British airmen, had been transferred on March 29, 1943, to the North Compound in Stalag Luft III.

It is here that a closed mouthed team of airmen begins plans for the biggest escape of the war. Soon your love is kept busy.

THE PERFECTIONIST

I bought Paul Brickhill's book *The Great Escape* to compare it with Jens's messages. I soon found out that Jens wrote very modestly about his own role in the escape preparations. For example, he simply says he belonged to the department that made the air pumps. According to Brickhill, Jens made the detailed drawings and built the pumps from scrap wood and leather scavenged from kitbags. Like Jens, the pumps proved reliable and effective.

Brickhill describes many other details about Jens's work that Jens doesn't think worth mentioning. For instance Jens made the seals used to stamp forged documents by carving eagles and swastikas into soap and casting the seals from melted silver foil.

For the buckles used on military disguises, Jens and a friend persuaded a guard to take off his jacket in the heat of the day. While the guard was distracted, Jens pressed the buckle into soap to make the mould. According to Brickhill, Jens's belt buckle "was perfect."

One request from the Escape Committee that seemed impossible even for Jens was to duplicate a carbine from wood that would be real enough to fool the guards at the camp's entrance. To get accurate measurements for the replica, Jens talked to a guard while another prisoner stood behind the guard measuring the real carbine with an improvised calliper. After carving the wood, Jens used nails and melted foil from cigarette packages to reproduce the metal parts. Then, as Brickhill writes, Jens "polished it with graphite until it was perfect." The carbine would be used in an almost successful escape by Jens's friend Per Berglund.

That was how the men in the camp viewed Jens—perfect. A perfectionist in everything he did. No mistakes.

"THEY WERE MISTAKEN"

The first two months in the new (north) camp were lively, not only because we were occupied getting our rooms and personal belongings in order, but also because attempts at escape were almost a daily occurrence. The queerest methods were tried just at the time when the Germans were busy organizing things in the new camp. They thought we were too busy getting our things in order to think of anything else.

They were mistaken.

...The main work started with the digging of three tunnels. All the experience gained from similar work in the old camp was put into it. The trapdoors leading down into the tunnel, which up to now had been the weak point which usually led to discovery of the tunnels were extremely carefully constructed. As it happened, the Germans themselves had been considerate enough to help us a long way with this. Contrary to the arrangement in the old barracks, a foundation was laid under each room in the new barracks. This consisted of a large square block which was meant to carry the weight of the oven and chimney. It was not difficult to find that the most convenient place for a tunnel entrance was just through such a foundation.

PRIDE AND PREJUDICE

August 30, 1943

Dearest,

It is exactly two months three days since I received a letter from you, & I am at a loss as to finding a reason. However another clothing parcel arrived on August 10th, all complete except for the notebooks. Thank you very much! With regards to letters, I am optimistic & trusting that the fall with its many rainy days will give you time enough to write me a note once in a while again. The very warm weather that has been prevailing these last four to five weeks has more or less put a stop to any serious reading or studying, although one book-parcel after another has arrived from England containing very good books indeed. Only some weeks ago I finished one of the first books you sent me, namely "Pride & Prejudice," which I enjoyed very much. — How is your work getting on Alice, & what are your thoughts nowadays? Your last letter was dated April 27 which makes the latest news I have of you four months old. — One Canadian whose companionship I value very much, his name is Donald McDonald, asks me if you know his friend Ruth Hanna, who lives in Lansdowne Ave 350. If you do, please give her his best regards. —

I am longing to see you again Alice.

Your Jens

You sent him *Pride and Prejudice*! And poker-faced Jens responds, "Which I enjoyed very much." Wouldn't Jane Austen have found her story of matrimonial manipulation an absolutely delightful coincidence considering all your complex Don and Jens misinterpretations? Will sweet Alice get her man in the end?

THE TUNNEL NAMED HARRY

"Harry's" entrance was made in barracks 104, in a room on the west side and at the northern end of the building. In this barrack each room had a small wrought-iron stove. The stove weighed 50 kilo and two men could lift it quite easily. It stood in the corner nearest the door. The floor in this corner was covered with tiles as protection against falling embers. The tile-covered area measured some 12 metre each way and rested on the brick foundation under the barrack. The Poles lifted out the tiles first. They then removed sufficient bricks from the middle of the foundation so that one man could get down into the hole quite comfortably, continuing until sand was reached.

The department to which I belonged was to be responsible for making three air pumps, and trolleys to carry sand from the tunnel face back to the shaft. All the Norwegians were employed in different other departments.

The weeks passed and "Tom" had now come so far that the work face was under the fence. Then it was discovered.

The Germans were triumphant and blasted the whole thing with dynamite. Like "Dick" and "Harry," "Tom" was constructed and equipped as solidly as possible. It was completely lined with wooden boards; it had electric light, trolleys running on rails for conveying personnel and sand, and an air pump to pump fresh air into the tunnel. The Germans were impressed and condescendingly complimented the prisoners on their good work. We gathered by what they said that they believed "Tom" was our only project of this kind. Which suited Big X just fine.

"Harry" had progressed farthest, but it was getting so late in the year that it could not be finished before winter and the bad weather set in. Work on "Dick" and "Harry" was therefore stopped, and the camp took more peaceful occupations.

Pete [Per Berglund] got a little "holiday" for fourteen days that Autumn, for going out of camp one evening after dark. Pete had been a student in Germany before the war and spoke the language very well, and was given a chance to attempt escape. Dressed as a German who daily patrolled the camp [with the wooden carbine Jens made him], he sauntered out of the camp when the guards were changing. All went well until a German guard who was going the same way wanted company and found out that something was wrong. They walked along together for a while but the German finally grew suspicious and Pete was nabbed.

When the New Year festivities were over "Big X" decided the time was ripe to start serious work again. All efforts should be centered on completing "Harry." In spite of the snow, work was started. During the long winter months this last great effort had been planned down to the minutest details, and a good deal of preliminary work done.

The main task was to dig the last 70 metres so quickly that even if the Germans suspected something was brewing they would not take action and come down on us before it was too late.

THE LAST SUMMER RIDE

My memories aren't date stamped. Like old photographs, they aren't easy to sort. Sometimes I find an event that I use as a marker, placing others before and after it. This story begins with this marker: The Trans-Canada Highway from Calgary to Banff was begun in 1957.

Before 1957, we drove to Canmore from Calgary along the narrow Highway 1A following the north side of the Bow River through Cochrane and west to Canmore.

That's how I remembered something special you did for me. In 1956 survey crews had marked a trail for the new highway from Canmore to Calgary.

I turn seven over the summer and Teddy is eleven. That fall we ride from Canmore to Calgary. I'm on Dolly and Teddy is on Twinkle and we're leading two other horses along the survey trail—just a narrow slash through chopped down spruce and fir, mudholes, and rock slides into creeks. On the first day we cross Dead Man's Flats where Mrs. McBride said the dead man had been found in the cabin by the corner of the meadow. Never look inside. The murderer will get you too. And Teddy for once treating me like I wasn't always difficult. But letting me lead on the trail sometimes and find the crossings over the creeks.

And there's your camp by a stream waiting for us. The station wagon loaded with supplies. Did we find you or did you find us? I never knew. The fire is smoking as we hobble and bell the horses. Dead men tired we joke. Tarp the saddles. Grin and act like there are no ghosts. Brush off the mosquitoes.

I see you now. A drink and a du Maurier. A frying pan on the fire. You who rode like a boy giving up your last summer mountain ride and are happy to see the doing it ourselves fun we are having. I remember your happiness.

I do not know how you got the station wagon there or how you found us every evening. I don't know the how or why of '56. All I know is that we made the ride to Calgary safely, two boys and four horses thanks to a mum who gave up her adventure to prove we could do it on our own.

Some mothers teach their children. You showed me I could do anything that summer.

That's how much you loved me and how much I loved you.

Learning to Ride. Too small to reach the stirrups, Tyler tucked his feet into the leathers and was ready for any adventure.

OF COURSE NOT

I had planned to tell you the last part of Jens and the Great Escape while sitting on a platform bench in the CPR's Calgary train station, our goodbye before your years of dying. I changed my mind at the last minute and now we're on the west edge of Calgary—where the tracks cross the Bow River. This is about as close to train stations as I like to get. You had an I'm not here look that afternoon. I never knew where you went.

On January 18, 1944, you write Jens an I still love you letter. However, you make it clear that when you are reunited you both may have changed. That will be the time to decide about your future together. It has been three years since you were last together. He will receive this letter in March while the prisoners are digging the last 330 feet of Harry. Jens has to think over his reply to you while he waits for the Escape Committee to choose the day for the escape and name the 200 men who will get a chance at freedom. What will he write if he is chosen? If he is not chosen? He can't hint about the escape. What if the worst happens? What should he say in his last letter to you?

Poker-faced Jens does not know the long odds he faces: 200 will try; only 76 will pass through the tunnel before the first shot is fired; 73 will be recaptured by early April. Of those, 50 would be executed by roadsides and in prisons while "attempting to escape." Only 3 will make it home.

If you knew the odds, would you have asked him to wait safely until the war was over?

He is thinking about what to write. About seeing you again. Holding you. About being together.

While he prepares, you spend your evenings in your room. Alone. Thinking about becoming a writer. Won't that be a knockout. All the stories, poems, and letters you've been working on won't be for nothing. Maybe a *New Yorker* story one day. But keep that dream to yourself. Keep Jens to yourself.

Big Marjorie has been relentless in her negotiations since you broke off the engagement to Don. Get married! Choose or I will. You still wonder how things got so out of hand with Don. And why it ended so badly at the party. He didn't deserve that. You kept all his love you letters. Not in an album like Jens's but you kept them.

Big Marjorie is in her bedroom. Sitting in her maroon velvet armchair that Bert says is a mistake. She is always suffering and always demanding. Her silver bell rings. Bring me this. Don't be so noisy. She never quits.

We're Tylers, Big Marjorie reminds you. Fine to do our part supporting the fighting men. We can entertain them. Show them what they are dying for. But marriage? Never. No foreigners. No artists. Nobody embarrassing. It's bad enough that you are wasting your time at McGill. What for? Who will you meet there?

She lines fresh suitors up for judgement. Thank you for the flowers. Sit down. Have a drink. What does your father do? Where do you live? No, Alice won't continue at McGill after she's married. Of course not.

Jens. His arms long since around you. Now eighteen months in Stalag Luft III. Will this war go on forever? I can hear your thoughts My Goodbye Mother who can't write about this. I will listen and I will write.

Does Jens know my loneliness? My despair? Each day is a battle to protect our secret. Marjorie suspects. Subtle devious questions. I bleed into my stories. Into my poems. Where can I find relief? So many lies to protect one promise.

I am 19. Almost 20. Still unmarried. Everybody asks what's wrong with me. Dad says I study too hard. What's my alternative? Marry somebody I don't love? Marry a name, an estate, a family fortune? Make my mother happy.

This McGill is new thinking. Wordsworth. The Romantics. The freedom of the individual. The French Revolution. Everyday man freed from chains. William Blake. ("To share with Tyler," you write years later in your book of romantic poetry and prose.)

Westmount Society. I can be freed from that. Freed from Big Marjorie's social climb to the top of Westmount Boulevard. Her pulpit to piss down on her world. I could find a life of poetry and love. Jens is poetry. Jens is love. Jens is outside the world of Westmount Alpine Inn debutantes coming out parties introductions family connections bank accounts and who's the most beautiful.

63 DAYS

ARRANGEMENTS

The 63 Days begin with a broken ankle and end with a broken heart.

You are skiing at the Alpine Inn. Bert and Big Marjorie are on the veranda watching the last races of the day. The slow afternoon snow is turning to fast ice as the last racers of the day prepare their skis. This is your chance to risk everything. To dare the speed Jens taught you. To win.

Day 1. March 9, 1944. The Alpine Inn

The sweeping drop above the lodge. Your skis chatter on the frozen ruts. They won't hold the turn. Too late. Crack! Your ankle breaks. You are shot down at the icy bottom of Hill 60.

Day 3. March 11, 1944. The Alpine Inn

There is a dance this evening. You are paired with strangers. Awkward. Ankle in plaster. Behind your blue eyes are tears. Behind your good evening how do you do smile the frustration clots and scabs. How much respectability can you endure?

A group of men are drinking in the lounge. You notice one in particular. Dark hair. Dark eyes. So unlike slender tall blond Jens. So unlike him. The dark one smiles catches your eye and raises his glass in polished acknowledgement.

He introduces himself. Sure of himself isn't he? Ted Trafford. A British engineer on holiday with his mother. Could she meet your parents...the Tylers...the owners of the Alpine Inn? He knows well the intricacies of the courtship ritual leading to a family alliance.

Day 3. March 11, 1944. Stalag Luft III

Jens receives your "I still love you" letter written January 18. He is reassured. The days of waiting are coming to an end.

Day 6. March 14, 1944. Stalag Luft III

The tunnel is within six inches of the surface. Big X calls a meeting of the Escape Committee. The breakout will take place on the moonless Friday night of March 24/25. We know the German trains will be running regular schedules on Saturday. Be on time. Don't attract attention.

Which men? Stalag Luft III holds over 10,000 men, all of whom want to escape. More than 600 have helped. The Escape Committee rules 220 will get the chance. The maximum that can make it through the tunnel before the morning roll call. The first 70 have been selected based on contribution and likelihood of success. The next 150 to be chosen by draw.

Jens is selected Number 13. Per Bergsland is Number 14. Good numbers. They'll be long gone before any alarm sounds.

Jens: wear your POW dog tags. "Stalag Luft 3 Nr. 296." The Germans shoot suspected spies.

Day 7. March 15, 1944. The Alpine Inn

The Trafford-Tyler matrimonial negotiations begin. Jens makes his preparations to waste no time coming to you. Big Marjorie encourages you to enjoy the parties at the Alpine Inn. Here's that British engineer again. Ted Trafford. Charming. Very suitable. He is staying three weeks.

Good evening, Mrs. Tyler. As beautiful as your daughter. Her eyelids flutter high in delight. He is so sophisticated. A blue blood.

Don't let a broken ankle spoil this evening. Let him sweep you off your feet. He has brought his mother to Quebec for a rest. Sigh. How wonderful it must be to have a son who takes you on vacation. I'm not well, you know. Sigh. Dance with him. So handsome. So polished. So presentable. I can always spot a Cambridge man.

Ted, Big Marjorie says her gunner eyes aimed, I would like to talk with your mother again. Sya. Such a delightfully Continental name. She wears her family crest splendidly. Show me your gold ring again. Edward LeMarchant

Trafford. Authentic French as well. Even better. I'm sure us mothers will get along. Come to some arrangement.

Now you two go and enjoy your young lives. You don't have forever.

Day 12. March 20, 1944. The Alpine Inn

Ted and his mother, Sya, are interested in Big Marjorie's proposition. They have six days of vacation left. They agree Ted will propose marriage.

DAY 12. MARCH 20, 1944

Jens writes his last letter to you from the camp. He has been a POW for 21 months. In four days he will be on his way to you. He must leave your sea stained photograph behind.

March 20, 1944

Dearest,

Your letter dated Jan 18th arrived here on Mar. 11th, & if you remember the contents of that letter you will appreciate my feelings. As a matter of fact, I have been waiting for such a letter from you for more than a year, & I was very glad to receive it, to say the least. Irrespective of that (whatever it is) which you refer to as having happened during these two years, what remains most important to me is the fact that you still remember me & the delightful times we spent in each others company well enough to write me such a letter as this last one. As you say Alice, owing to these long years of separation nothing can be sure regarding our feelings towards each other before we meet again. But then it is wrong of me to ask you to wait like this, because I might then appeal to some feeling in you that has nothing to do with love & affection. Therefore your letter was a very great relief in many ways. —Alice dear, I wish I could tell you that I have very definite plans as to the future after the war, plans which are as ambitious as I imagine you would like them to be & consequently would form a fairly substantial basis for your faith in me, but my plans do not amount to more than what I have already told you in previous letters. But those plans I am going to carry through with the necessary modifications to make them practicable.—You once taught me that I could get anything I wanted badly enough & that the main thing for us was to have faith in each other. Anyhow Alice, these waiting years seem to be at their end & I promise I shall not waste any time in coming to you then.

  With all my love I remain,

Your Jens

As always, he offers his love without terms. Not a word about the tunnel. One promise—"Anyhow Alice, these waiting years seem to be at their end & I promise I shall not waste any time in coming to you then."

  Ahead of Jens is . . . Shot whilst trying to escape. But there is also you, Dearest Alice. For you he will risk his life. He is Your Jens and he will not waste any time in coming to you.

DAY 16. MARCH 24, 1944

On the morning of March 24th our "marshal" came and gave us the code word: "Tonight's the night."

I had waited for this a long time and was prepared for it, still, when I heard it a cold shiver ran down my back. All during the day I noticed a new, tense and expectant expression on the faces of my companions. The thought of leaving this hated god-forsaken place made us go about as in a dream. But, at the same time, peace came to our thoughts. After the intense period of waiting and preparation it was good at last to know that now it was going to happen, and to concentrate on it.

There were many more smiling faces to be seen about than usual. But of course there were those whose preparations were not yet completed and their faces did not look exactly peaceful. I myself was getting a sixpence cap ready.

After lunch we received our papers. I had expected them to be well made out, but had never dreamed they would be so perfect. Even though I knew that each of the five papers I received were false and made by hand I could scarcely detect the swindle.

It was 12:30 before Pete and I Nos. 14 and 13 respectively were ordered into the corridor to stand in readiness to go down the shaft. Those who were still in their rooms at 12 o'clock, when all lights went out, had been told to turn in. Boots and equipment remained in the corridor, to avoid rummaging and noise in the dark rooms. The atmosphere was charged with excitement, the marshals' low-toned orders and quick, stealthy footsteps going back and forth along the corridor did not relieve the tension. The marshals were at this time short tempered and got worked up at the slightest impediment of traffic through the tunnel. Orders were given that those who were found to be overloaded and too bulky after the last check would be forbidden to go through.

Pete and I sat quite close to the door leading into the room where the shaft was. One by one men disappeared through the door, but we could not see the room from where we sat. Something or other started worrying my middle regions. I could hardly sit still. At last my turn came. I got up and went through the door. Four cupboards stood in front of the window so the light from the kerosene lamps would not be seen outside. The shaft descended in one corner of the room. The marshal checked my kit for the last time. All day they had been considering my suitcase and wondering if I could take it through with me. But, I climbed down the ladder with the suitcase on my shoulder, and noticed nothing wrong. Three men were waiting at the bottom of the shaft, so I had to hang on to the ladder before going right down. Then I was told to wait in the discharge room, and this took a couple minutes. My middle regions had quieted. I was no longer nervous. The trolley returned. I put my suitcase in front on the trolley rails, crawling on behind and wriggled into place. A few seconds later I lay comfortably on my stomach on the trolley, grabbed the trunk with outstretched arms and lifted it in front of me. Then I ducked my head and gave the "all clear" signal.

…Apparently the length of the tunnel had been miscalculated to the extent that the exit shaft had surfaced just short of the tree line and not well into the woods as intended. Therefore each man would be plainly visible as he emerged and ran across the open bit which separated him from the shelter of the trees.

This danger made it necessary to post a marshal outside to tell each escapee when the coast was clear. The marshal was posted just within the trees. He could signal to the tunnel exit by means of a thin rope laid out on the ground. Each escapee would without emerging from the shaft tell the marshal: "I'm here" by one pull on the rope. The marshal would then signal back "wait" or "come" whatever would fit the movements of the Germans.

I lifted the suitcase onto my shoulder and began climbing up the ladder. This shaft was narrower than the descent in the barrack but I managed to get out of it without a hitch. Just before reaching the top I recognized the signalling rope which was fastened to one of the top rungs. I grabbed the rope and pulled it. Waited for an answer but got none. I pulled again and this time received a reply: "All clear."

I could see the clear sky above me and small stars indistinctly through the night mist. I climbed up and found my head above the ground. I turned towards the camp and was startled: one of the watch-towers was not more than thirty meters away. The watchman up there was apparently very keen, because he kept on looking in the direction of the camp. As long as he did this we could feel safe. I crawled right up onto the snow-covered ground, and with the guiding rope in my hand walked quickly into the woods.

DAY 21. MARCH 29, 1944

Marjorie questions you.

Yes. I accepted.

Good. Sya and I have agreed a three-month engagement will be appropriate.

DAY 21. MARCH 29, 1944

Jens and Per have arrived by train in Stettin, a German-held port where Swedish sailors helped them stowaway on their ship sailing the next day for neutral Sweden. They had one dangerous trial left to pass — the ship would be searched by German patrols before it left the harbour. "Cold sweat poured out of me."

We heard the hatch open and someone coming down the ladder. Voices, German voices. Now we heard the German say: "Was ist dar?" A loud, angry voice. And we heard our friend answer; — "Nothing." The German mumbled: "Na, ich will nach sehmn." (I will see.) After which we heard him climbing over the bulkhead to the chain case. All we could do was hold our breath. Cold sweat poured out of me. I heard him swear under his breath as he crawled over the slippery chain and over to the bulkhead of the rubbish case. I heard him breathing and growling as he came nearer. Then his torch touched the iron bulkhead which separated him from us. Then he bent down and felt something we had over us. I lay between two rolls of netting and suddenly felt his hand on my shoulder. I held my breath, tried not to tremble, and was sure he could hear my heart beating. Then he let go with a: "Na gut" and the light disappeared.

I heard him climb back over the chain and soon afterwards they both went up the ladder again. The hatch was closed and we thought we were alone once more, but could not be quite certain, so waited awhile before whispering to each other and discussing what to do next. We agreed to lie low for some time yet, because the Swede had told us that the ships had another inspection at the outlet of the harbour.

Five or six hours later:

We peeped out of the porthole and saw light.

"Light!" — "lots of light!" Sweden!

I felt like shouting with joy but would probably have disturbed the police who were checking our papers.

In 1951, six years after the war ended, Paul Brickhill would write of Jens and Per's accomplishment: "It was the perfect escape."

DAY 22. MARCH 30, 1944

The Alpine Inn

Friends phone the Alpine Inn. Congratulations. Ted's sooooo right for you. We just loooove his British accent. We heard he's going to take you to Venezuela. How terribly exciting.

Thank you. And you do not say, I will continue my writing. And you do not ask, will there be time for that in Venezuela? Away from Big Marjorie there will be time. You believe.

Betty Goodfellow phones: "Be careful. Ted won't be good for you." She does not know about Jens. Nobody does.

Sweden

Jens and Per are free men! In Stockholm, they are interrogated by the British Counsel before arrangements are made for their return to England.

DAY 24. APRIL 1, 1944. NEW YORK

The engagement settled, Ted leaves for the Shell Oil offices in New York where he attends a friend's wedding and writes:

Dear Alice,

...Feel a bit better now after about 10 hours sleep and a bath! That's the trouble with wedding parties and receptions. They made me be an usher so I got the low down on everything. All those things you have to promise in the service are pretty grim! Have you ever listened carefully to a wedding service? I was quite scared! Hope you and I will be able to live up to it all when our turn comes!

...All my love and see you soon, my sweetheart,

Ted

Didn't you wonder? Why would he warn his fiancée that he might have trouble keeping the "pretty grim" marriage vows? Did Jens ever falter?

HESITATION

Day 31. April 8, 1944. London

Jens and Per are flown to England. He sends telegrams. "I am longing to see you Alice. Love your Jens Müller."

I cannot imagine what you thought. To me, your reading this telegram must have been like the moment when Santiago saw the marlin's immensity swimming under the skiff, longer than the skiff. Can a marlin be that big? Never. But he is.

And Jens has escaped from his never and is coming for you.

You hesitate. You delay announcing your engagement on the Society Page. You see the sharks closing in on you. Big Marjorie suspects her plan is in trouble. She presses you. Quit McGill. Get ready for your marriage. We want to see the Trafford Family crest on your little finger.

Day 42. April 19, 1944. Venezuela

Sya presses her son. We're broke. Marry the rich blonde. Secure our future.

Ted writes from Venezuela. "Why haven't you announced the engagement yet?"

DAY 53. APRIL 30, 1944. LONDON

Dearest!

Thanks for your answer to my telegram. It took less than a week to reach me, & the distance between us seems quite small again.

Although it makes me feel like a recruit waiting to be examined by a medical board, I agree with you that we shall have to meet again before we make up our minds to marry; I mean: "who to marry."

It's all very difficult, isn't it? With the best years flying past, & nothing happening; & the memories fading, etc.

I only hope Alice, that you do not feel bound by the things you told me when you were seventeen. It is unfair to your-self to wait for a fellow like me, whose future is very uncertain.

Well Alice, I shall end this letter now by telling you that I love you more than ever, & ask you to please send me a big photo of yourself (Ottar says you have changed a lot). You see, I had to leave (in Stalag Luft III) the one you gave me in Canada.

My love to all of you.

Your Jens

Your Jens is a gentleman. All he asks for is a photograph. He will not hold you to the promise you made before he was stationed in England. He will wait and see.

Now he is doing what he promised—he is not wasting any time in coming to you. He is crossing the Atlantic on a troop ship. On board, he hears the terrible news—50 of his fellow prisoners were executed after the escape, including fellow Norwegian Halldor Espelid. Only he, Per Berglund, and a Dutchman, Bram van der Stok, had made it home.

DAY 63. MAY 10, 1944. EDEN BROOK

And now I'm here, thinking of you 62 years later. Thinking of your blue eyes, your strong hands, and your thick wave of blonde hair and all the things we stopped talking about after our railway station goodbye. Yours was the hardest silence I will ever know. Your blue eyes and thick wave of blonde hair are fine grey ashes buried below two square feet of echoing bronze.

Flight Lieutenant Jens Müller rides his Norton motorcycle into your debutante world. The shot down Spitfire pilot. Escaped from Stalag Luft III. Handsome. Modest. Offering you no future but his love forever.

"I am promised to another," you tell Your One Good Thing.

Those are your words. Verbatim. You repeated them years later to a close to your hidden heart friend. She gave them to me.

"I am promised to another."

Sixty years later I attend your funeral not knowing about an album. About The Campbell's Soup Box you packed for me. Not knowing you were tied to me by this:

"A fisherman like Santiago keeps his truly big fish in his heart, whether he brings it to the shore or not. What or who we love never gets away. We fight the sharks forever to remember that love."

163

TERMS OF AN ENGAGEMENT

THE HARD FACTS

The Holy Cross Hospital is closed now. Out of date. But a good place for us to talk. Five of your seven children born here. I too often drove you to the entrance in 1977 for your cobalt treatments. One breast. Your womanness under attack by surgeons and infidelity. Your thick blonde hair thin and dry. Slipping a couple of joints into your pack of du Mauriers. Stopped the nausea you said.

I didn't bring you today to see this sadness vacant parking lot. Only so I could remember the hard muscles along your jaw the day you said it always hurt. You wake up knowing it is going to hurt all day. Nothing can be done about it. Endure. I was enduring but not like you. You were so goddamned strong.

I'll read this 1977 letter from your suitcase.

Dear _____

I haven't written you since before Xmas. The effect of the cobalt is wearing off now & I am not feeling so tired and depressed. Also I am in the hands of an excellent cancer doctor. He wants me to use chemotherapy starting the 1st of March but will watch it for a few days after the treatment which takes four days & then stop it if it is too disastrous.

Alice

Your cancer was unavoidable so you endured the pain, fighting back with your fuck you attitude. But with Ted you endured a pain you didn't have to. Why no fighting back? Was never going back the only way you knew to live?

I cannot reconcile the cancer fighting you with the strange to me hint of acquiescence in the Terms of An Engagement letters you wrote Ted after he had returned to Venezuela for the seemly three-month waiting period.

Or did you already see the black eyes ahead? The marriage deal done, the promise made. Could you guess but not believe what was to come for the Golden Girl? You were now his. To do with as he feudally pleased. Cancer must have seemed of no concern to you.

Your family has plans for a grand Montreal wedding. The demands begin. Ted wants to be married in Trinidad with his mother and father. You write:

May 11, 1944

Ted darling,

Tonight I sent you a cable saying how much Mummy and Daddy wish us to be married up here at our home if possible. Under ordinary circumstances, my mother, and perhaps everyone, might easily have gone down to Trinidad with me, but as you probably know only my father would be able to go down.

Ted darling you must know how much I love all my family and it means more than I can tell you to have them at our wedding. They have all told me it would be a great disappointment to them if they could not be there too.

…The date of our wedding will be up to you to decide and since, in all probability, it will take place up here, I hope that it will still be in July or August. We could be married either in Montreal or St. Marguerite's—would you like to be married in St. Marguerite's? I think that perhaps that would be the best but that again would be up to you. I know that Mummy would arrange for it to be really lovely up here and that both you and I would have many happy memories in the future. However, there will be no plans made until you let me know what can and cannot be done.

Ted darling, forgive me if I am being selfish in telling you how I

feel about this. You must know that the only important part to me is
that I love you so very much that I would go to any lengths to make
you happy.

...I realize that even if you are more to me than anyone else in the
world I still owe a great deal to the others I love. But it is not only
because my family want us to be married here but also because I want
to be with them. And so again darling, forgive me, but may we be
married at our home?

...All my love

Alice.

The apologetic tone of this letter isn't like you. Not at all. Ted's harsh response
was undated and without a salutation:

Just received three letters and also a cable about your family suggesting
that we be married at your home if suitable. Now for some hard
facts re this latter! Between us, darling, there can be no reticence or
concealments of the facts of any case; there is no need for me to tell
you how much I appreciate the spirit in which your parents make
this suggestion, but I do feel that it is impractical for the following
reasons: —

1. It is war-time and we are terribly short-staffed and while I could
insist on special leave I wouldn't feel quite right about it just having
come back from foreign leave. To Trinidad, as opposed to Canada, is
an easy hop. I can wait till you are there first [and settle] the exact date
of my leaving until fairly late and be the minimum time travelling and
the maximum time honeymooning in Caracas or somewhere! If I take
10 days to go to Canada and back most of the time will be dashing in
and out of trains, planes and hotels, and we might be held up for days
waiting for priorities.

2. The money position. You get your fares paid by the company,
but special leave is for personal account. There and back will cost
about $750 for me. Now I could if necessary afford this amount, but
it seems to me a lot better to spend such a sum later if for example
you want to take a trip back home after being down here a year or so.

I don't believe I ever told you about the financial situation. You had better know the facts. My salary is $400 (U.S.) a month. We then get a living allowance of about $180 (married). The latter takes care of food and servants o.k. as far as I can gather. Of course, house, gas, light, etc. furniture, medical care, here and any treatment needed abroad, are on the company. Taxes are negligible. After paying your provident fund (10% of your salary to which the company adds 10%) and club bills have been deducted, we will probably receive $250-300 per month in the bank in the USA. One never sees any money here. The accounts department makes all the deductions and you get a piece of paper with your monthly statement. You will begin to understand why often in Canada I never had any change! You just get used to not thinking about cash! So now you have a rough idea of your future financial level. But it is hard to compare with what you'd have at home. The way of living is so different. Afraid I've never saved anything. i.e. all spent on leaves except for a few war bonds and my provident fund. Bad, I know, but since I was at school my parents have been comfortably well-off and I never got in the habit of thinking about rainy days!! And in this sort of job, nowadays, you can be reasonably secure, and if you get fired you'd not have much difficulty getting another job, and then always more or less unconsciously at the back of one's mind is the knowledge that one's family wouldn't let one starve. People who have been poor are generally a lot more careful than people like us. I guess it is a question of the fact that these things are only learned the hard way—by experience. Well, you and I will have to start learning together. Open a savings account or something!

That was quite a digression about money, wasn't it? So back to site of wedding. I know that the reasons I think we ought to get married in Trinidad are rather practical ones. Against those are the feelings and desires of your parents and maybe your own. Also I told you that if you really wanted me to come to Canada, one way or another, I would. That still goes. So in the light of the above let me know if you are happy for it to take place in Trinidad.

I know my parents will make you absolutely at home for the time you will be with them. I don't quite gather whether <u>all</u> of our parents expect us to wait longer till some time in July. It will be more than three months in mid-July; after all I think that anyone would be convinced by then that we know our minds! My love, my only desire is to be with you. I know you feel the same. For goodness sake don't let's have any hold ups unless absolutely unavoidable. Maybe we are being a little selfish, but on the other hand our parents will see us fairly often, and in an emergency it is only a couple of days journey to Canada.

About the ring; I have already written you and to confirm it sent a cable today. Must close as this is from the office and I have a stack of company letters to sign.

All my love, my own Alice, Ted.

And so ends the lesson: 838 words about hard facts, 7 words about love. How many lies are twisted into those facts… "my parents have been comfortably well off."

You agree to be married, without your family, in Trinidad.

As for the engagement ring, Bert took care of it, buying a diamond for you at Birks in Montreal. Ted would later pay half the Birks bill when pressed by Bert. Ted's parents gave Alice a gold ring with the Trafford family crest.

JENS'S LAST TO ALICE

Now, My Goodbye Mother, you are committed to your choice. You have dropped out of McGill. You are married. You will carry The Jens Album with you all over the world as you follow Ted to the oil fields of South America, Egypt, Ecuador, California, Canada, and Australia.

Your last letter from Jens is tucked into a corner of the Album's back cover. He must be on good terms with Big Marjorie, now that you are married and in Venezuela! And even he is using dashes. I bet he learned that from you.

August 3, 1944

Dear Alice,

This is my first letter to you since you left. By the time you receive it you will be married; so I wish you all the happiness in the world Alice. —

How was your trip to Trinidad? I bet you enjoyed every minute of it, as only you can.

Your father told me you had a spot of trouble with the weather on the way to New York. However judging by your mother's report on how you spent the fourteen days there, the rough trip could not have affected you much. —

Remember I am anxiously looking forward to hearing from you soon please, yes?? —

Oil Field Life, California. No matter how often Alice moved the family with
Ted, from Egypt to Ecuador, she never lost track of her Jens Album.

Please excuse the pencil, You see it is too late to get hold of some
ink and I want to get this letter off tomorrow morning. —

I am now busily occupied at learning my future profession:
Teaching (pilot training)! — I still don't smoke. (pretty good, eh?) I
still visit the Inn although I don't like it as well as I did before. I spent
three days there about a week ago before starting work. During which
three days my boudoir was No. 3 at the Golf Club and my room
mates were drunk most of the time. Great life. However, my attitude
towards mankind is always friendly when I am at the Inn; so nothing
happened. Next time I go North I'll avail myself of your mother's
invitation to stay in John's house.

Write soon as you promised.

                                                Jens.

CONSEQUENCES

A CONFIDENTIAL CONVERSATION

I talked this week with a friend of yours. "G." I'd often seen her name in your notes. Your circling handwriting on the calendar. Initials on a *New Yorker* cover. In the intermittent fragments of your diaries. I told her how puzzling your life was to me. I am working on understanding it. Still. Two years after the funeral.

We sat in her study. She had a glass of wine. Her husband had a Scotch. She knew you a lot better than I suspected. You were a difficult friend especially with women. I could name your women friends on one hand. Helen. Hildegard. Judy. Virginia. Betty. And now I add G.

I began by telling her about The Jens Album and my visit to Montreal. I wanted to be clear about what I had learned so far. Like your friends and your brother, G. didn't recognize Jens's name. But you had told her that there had been somebody you had loved before Ted. A lot. The Album didn't surprise her. Everyone she says has a secret love in their life. Someone they left behind. (Her husband looked up for a moment when she said this.) Then they get married and the past love fades away. The letters and photos fade. There's no reason to keep them.

So why did Alice hide The Jens Album for 60 years? Why did she give it to me without an explanation?

G. held her face in her hands. Thinking. She's a graceful woman. I remember her movie star gorgeous as a young woman. Today she is a handsome grandmother. In control of her emotions. Behind her hands this evening I wonder if the control is there. She sits up. Straight. Elegant. She glances at her husband then begins.

Alice and Ted were in love when they came to Calgary. Alice looked at Ted with stars in her eyes. She adored him. Everybody could see it. Alice was so full of life. Doing everything for Ted and her children. The perfect family.

We noticed Ted didn't help her. He liked to sit in the living room with the guests while Alice fed the children and made dinner. Lots of men were like that in those days. Alice kept having babies. She always seemed to be pregnant or feeding one. Ted was charming and popular. He didn't seem to enjoy having the children around. Alice would be on the floor laughing and playing with the children and Ted would be annoyed.

Then we saw Ted out with a young lady. It was so wrong. Alice was at home taking care of the family and he was out with this girl spending money. We knew they didn't have a lot of money.

That was when Alice and I began to talk. It was terrible for her. Always pregnant. Losing at least two. And she knew about Ted. We would go riding together. Or she would come here and let the children play in the yard while we talked. I don't know how many women were involved with him. All their friends gossiped.

Alice would always tell me she wouldn't break up the family. Her children were more important than anything else to her. The family had to stay together.

Alice was committed to the marriage and the family. She was going to see it through. I think Alice was mentally the strongest person I have ever known. She would not give up. She would not quit. She had opportunities to get her own back. She could have had men and done what she wanted but she didn't. She didn't think that way.

The drinking was a gradual thing. Sometimes she had too much to drink. It might have been in the early 1960s that we noticed it was a problem.

G. pauses as I stand 13 years old on the railway platform. Early 1960s.

G. smiles at me. But Alice was fun. She could make us laugh. What a sense of humour. We wanted to see her but it got to be too difficult. I wish now I had gone to see her more often.

When she was diagnosed with cancer and was in pain she never complained. Never. Not once. She just took it. That was how strong she was.

She never complained. Not about your father. Not about money. Not about the cancer. She loved her family and nothing could change that.

What about Jens and the Album?

What do you think Tyler?

I answer, I think she kept the Album as a memory. Not something she was going to do anything about. As a memory that at one time in her life somebody loved her. Loved her for herself. Jens didn't want anything. Not the Tyler family money. Not the Alpine Inn. Not her looks. He just loved her.

She agrees. You're right she says.

And why did she leave it to me without an explanation?

G. puts her face in her hands again. Composing her thoughts. Then her eyes holding me, she says: "She wanted you to understand. She didn't care if anybody else did. But she wanted you to know. Showing it to you or giving you an explanation would have taken away its meaning for you. You had to find all this out for yourself to really understand her."

I say goodbye. Not much else to say. Small talk. I drive half a block and stop.

My face is wet. I'm sorry Mum. I wanted too much from you. I wanted you to always be the way you were. I wanted that forever. I could never endure pain the way you did.

ON THE WAY TO TRINIDAD

Here's a writing the way you talk letter of yours that I enjoyed. You sent it from New York, on your way to be married in Trinidad. It's full of random thoughts. I can hear you in every phrase. By the way, I still have the voice recording we made just before you died. It's full of dashes, too. And truths I can't delete.

July 13, 1944

Dearest Mum,

Just a short note before I go out shopping—Last night we got tickets for Oklahoma! Can you believe it? The show was marvellous—we enjoyed every minute in spite of our fears that it couldn't possibly come up to expectation—It was better!

Yesterday Dad and I managed to see everything from the Police Department to the oldest church in town—Trinity Church. There were tombstones in the yard dating as far back as 1732! And probably even further—a lot of them were half buried and you couldn't read the blurred inscriptions. The Venezuelan Counsel was something! Wait till Dad tells you about it. To top everything they had to be bribed to do the job. The police cost us $4.00!—Imagine!

After the show last night we went to the Stork Club. Mrs. Orr was there—remember her from Holts? I don't know what or who they thought we were, but all evening they kept bringing drinks to our table: "On the house" — we're going back!

I meant to tell you yesterday that after we came out of "Leon and Eddies" we walked back to our hotel — and on the way we wandered through St. Patrick's Church.

By the way it was very fitting for us to see Oklahoma — there was a wedding for the climax! Put us in the mood — or me at least — for what's coming — my goodness I am happy. Poor dad. I think I talked both his ears off last night — you know me and my philosophies!

All my love darling to you and the kids,

Alice

P.S. Can you read my poor excuse for writing! — something eh?

As I transcribed your letters between you and your parents I noticed one of your many punctuation idiosyncrasies that I had long forgotten. The dash — you and your parents use it like a pause in your thoughts — as if you can't slow down — and suddenly here's another thought. The dash must have been embedded in me because for years I would get copy back from editors with dozens of my dashes replaced by conventional punctuation — like periods and semicolons, eh.

TEA WITH DAD

I'm trying to understand you and Dad. Understand the "what happened" of your marriage. The consequences. I'll have to ask him about 1944 and that's bothering me. I'm still stuck at you marrying him and with my always wondering what he's planning next for me. I can't remember the last time we agreed on anything, other than to be polite.

He's 89 and as healthy as ever. He lives alone. He doesn't read because his eyes are bad—macular degeneration. He wants to live the last years of his life in the condo of your last years. Nursing homes and hospitals frighten him. Rather than give in to his poor eyesight he's learned his way through corridors by constantly touching familiar corners of tables, stairs, chairs, railings, and countertops. He knows where everything is in the kitchen. He can cook and take care of himself.

Did he know about your engagement to Jens? Maybe it's not a polite question.

I phoned earlier to say I would be dropping by. I didn't give a reason and he didn't ask. When you're 89 you probably look forward to any company. Even that difficult Tyler. I wonder what he wants.

As I walk up the steps, I haven't decided if I'll ask about Jens. I push the doorbell. He opens the door and I see him for the first time as an old man. He waits for me to speak, so he'll know it's me by my voice. There's no squeeze left in his handshake. He's slightly stooped but steady on his feet. Every thought I've had about him in the past 44 years drifts away. Every thought but one. Sadness.

The only question I want to ask, I can't — Do you know the wonder of Mum's truly big fish?

Or are you a tourist idly curious about the high finned backbone swaying in the harbour shallows. Of no consequence.

Or are you one of the sharks?

That's all I want answered. But we have this truce and I'm not going to break it. I'll be polite and see where conversation leads us. He says: I'll put the kettle on the hob. He's very British these days. As he makes the tea he asks about my family. Judy. Our children Nicolas and Sharnee Alice. His grandchildren. Our granddaughter Bailey. His first great-grandchild.

We talk on faded velvet armchairs. His black leather slippers have shuffled a path of safe familiarity through toast crumbs and carpet threads. The phone ringing upstairs not heard. He cups his palm behind his hearing aid offering me a biscuit. I hadn't noticed the tremor in his hand before. His gold family ring loose on his thin finger.

Strange to me this faded velvet conversation. He talks of working in Venezuela during the war as a petroleum engineer for Shell. His mother Sya and father, also named Edward/Ted, living in Trinidad.

He says: My father was in charge of an oil field. He had hoped to stay on a family farm in South Africa but couldn't. Fortunately some military friends had given him this job in Trinidad. My parents never even owned their own home. They had no security. I remember his hard facts letter to you when he wrote that his parents were comfortably well off. I had some time off work and I chose the Laurentians for a holiday and I invited my mother. My brother, John, had been missing in action since the Battle of El Alamein (Egypt) in September 1942.

He talks about his mother's search for John, the letters, the not knowing. It reminds me of Ottar Malm's shot down letter to you. Grief everywhere. The shrapnel scars of loved ones lost. Second Lieutenant E.J. Trafford. (Same rank as Jens.) Last seen running toward a truckload of mines. Presumed dead after one of Rommel's shells hit the truck. Buried as an unknown. Or is he a POW?

He says: My parents spent almost everything they had on our education. My brother and I were their only hope for their future. (No wonder Sya and Big Marjorie got along so well, I think but do not say.) My brother and I left South Africa when we were boys to go to boarding school in England.

My brother and I went to Cambridge. My brother and I were engineers. He joined the army as an engineer and went overseas. I joined Shell.

When my brother was reported missing in Egypt my mother was in despair. She never really recovered from not knowing what had happened to him. I was all she had left. That's why I brought her with me to the Laurentians. That was March 1944. My brother's grave wasn't found until 1945.

He says: We had only been at the Alpine Inn for a day or two when I met Alice. We danced. Her ankle was in a cast. A skiing accident. We fell in love and decided to get married. Our mothers thought we should wait before the wedding date was announced. I had to go back to Venezuela.

We each have another biscuit. I am my own witness to his circuitous memories of you and him. What was Alice's mother like? I ask. Big Marjorie I think but do not say.

Marjorie? Wonderful. Very helpful to me. I loved her. I needed to shop in Montreal for underwear and socks before I left and asked her to suggest a store. She said the Tylers didn't shop. The stores sent everything to the Tyler house. The next day Morgan's Department Store sent a man around with a selection of underwear and socks for me to choose from.

He talks of Bert's plans to share his businesses with you some day. He says Bert had hopes for you. The marriage changed those plans. His half smile acknowledges the possibility things might have been different.

"We only knew each other a few weeks," he says acknowledging other possibilities.

Teddy was born in Trinidad. Ted Jr.

Then a second pregnancy he recalls you sweating in the Venezuelan jungle and saying there is no need to call a plane. Just a stomach ache. Delaying until the superintendent insists you need more than field diagnosis and home remedies. The short runway and long operation in Maracaibo. Almost died. An ectopic pregnancy. Long years afterwards you make the oil company rounds of London New York Montreal Cairo doctors. Always the same news. Don't expect more children. Consequences of choices. Alice made choices. I made choices. We both made mistakes. That was our marriage. That was our life together.

He brushes his hand over his eyes forgetting he is wearing glasses.

Awkward. The tears I don't see. Tremors tap his ring against the table.

Strange to me to see how gently he holds your experience. The continuum of your life together has merged all his instances smooth as a silk globe of time and place. The whole of your marriage is all his thin gold ringed fingers can safely support. No emerald details to slip through his tremors. No good times. No bad times. No ruby shining specifics. No need to fix askew glasses. That was our life together.

Even though we only knew each other for a few weeks our marriage outlasted many others. That's something I'm proud of. We both did some silly things but we stayed married until the end.

He looks me in the eye. My look replies I won't break the truce over silly things.

More tea? he asks.

The kettle is on the hob the next month when I come back to continue the conversation.

I've been reading some of the letters and notes Mum left me. I wish I had more. I'd like to know more about her.

He passes me the biscuits. There are a couple of filing boxes you could look through.

Oh. Where?

They're locked in the storage room in the basement.

Could I get them out?

I'd have to make a special arrangement with the front desk of the condo.

I'd like to see what's in the boxes.

There's not much.

Is there anything about Mum's family?

I don't think so. I can't remember.

I phone him later in the week. No. He hasn't had time to talk to the front desk. It's coming up to the Calgary Stampede. The staff at the front desk are too busy to take you to the storage room.

The tea is on the hob after Stampede and we talk again about my family. Then I say I've found something interesting in the things Mum left me. Did she ever mention Jens Müller to you?

No.

He was a Norwegian she knew at the Alpine Inn.

Must have been before she met me.

That might be true. Or a lie. I have no trust in his words. I say, Jens was one of the men who escaped from Stalag Luft III.

I phone Dad a week later. He's glad I called. He says it would be a good idea if I had a look in your boxes. He suggests I might like to write something about you and your family. Like the research he did on the Trafford family.

The next day he gives me the keys to the storage room. Down I go. There has to be fifty Trafford inheritance boxes in the vault. He loves his Magna Carta genealogy. It gives an aristocratic tone to crested silver spoons and diamond wedding rings and the Anne Boleyn's ring nonsense story told to frighten sleepy children. Taken from her finger before her beheading ordered by the King. Not so sleepy children then. Truce I tell myself as I take out the two boxes of Tyler family history. Be polite. Quiet.

Some folders look promising. Alpine Inn. Papers from Little Marjorie's apartment. Flanagan family photographs. My heart bounces. This is where The Jens Album should have been. Why did you give it to me?

I phone Dad. I'd like to do some genealogical work on the Tyler family Dad. It might make an interesting addition to the work you've done on the Trafford family. Not as important but just for the record.

That's a good idea.

Would it be okay if I kept the boxes with Mum's papers awhile longer?

Yes. Use anything you want. Keep them as long as they are useful.

Thanks Dad.

We share a faded velvet truce.

AND WHERE WAS TED?

Ted never showed up for the birth of their first child. He just let Alice head off from Venezuela to Trinidad where his parents could take care of things.

December 2, 1945

Dearest Mum and Dad,

I arrived in Trinidad safe and sound, on Thursday night. The trip over was long but not rough. The plane came in an hour late. The exciting part of my trip was actually coming out of Casigua. There are two ways of getting out of that part of the world — one by plane and secondly by trolley, a square wheeled vehicle that guarantees to bounce off five pounds at the minimum. From there you have to spend twenty-two hours on a tanker twisting and turning all down the Rio Tara and Zulia until you reach the Maracaibo Lake. In the dry season — May, June, July — the boat gets stuck on the river banks regularly and it is a matter of three or four days before the trip is completed.

Well, up until Wednesday there had been no plane for three weeks. No mail, no nothing from the civilised world!! The regular pilot was ill and could not fly. The R.C.A.F. pilot could not speak Spanish and so was not allowed to fly according to Venezuelan law. You can imagine the excitement — me ready to produce any time and no way out of Casigua. I wasn't the least bit worried — I imagine I could have made the trolley-boat trip alright although it wasn't a pleasant expectation. Well "old Joe Shell" came through in the end. They whisked the R.C.A.F. pilot through a Spanish test and sent a special plane to get me. The rumours that went around Maracaibo were very funny — people were asking who it was that had to be rushed out of Casigua in such a desperate rush — some even thought the baby had arrived en route. However it was only me and there was no mishap. I stayed overnight with the Lucie-Smith's — Ted's boss in Maracaibo and they were very nice. They took me to the plane the next morning and the Watsons also came to see me off.

Yesterday I went to see Dr. Swart and he pronounced me 100%!!! Good news what!!! Furthermore, in about another two weeks I should have a fine healthy baby and what do you think of that? I am half excited and half scared — It's all very well when the baby is safely tucked away — but what does one do after that!!?! I can imagine the first time I am left alone and the baby starts to cry. I know I shall grab it and charge to the nearest capable person.

Now I have a favour to ask again! I did try to find something to send Joanie from Ted and I for this big debut. There was nothing, however, absolutely nothing in Maracaibo that was worthwhile. So I wonder whether you would choose something in Birks for me Mother. I think a silver bracelet would be nice (around $25) — can you do that? We do want her to have it special — maybe she has seen something she likes. Tell her I am sorry that we could not send something from here. (You send the bill to me for sure, sure and I will send a cheque return.)

I guess everyone is all excited about Joanie's party now — I know how nice it will be. It would be fun if we could be there too. And then right after that is Christmas. — Are you going up north? — I am so d--- annoyed that my good things all come at once. Baby and Christmas are right on top of each other — poor management I guess!

I have received two letters since I have been here from you — am looking forward to more. As soon as the baby is born you will receive a cable. I have heard that it is possible to telephone now —

Do you know if this is true?—I remember when we thought we could telephone Venezuela and couldn't.—Ted is very well—but pretty worried about this baby business—I know he will be awful glad when we get back.

Well that's all my news for the moment. I will write again soon.

All my love to all of you—

And kisses

Your Alice

THE GOLDEN GIRL

What's comforting about your graveyard is the absence of normality. At Eden Brook everybody talks and nobody listens.

The veteran sways, twisting his hands and twisting his hands and twisting his hands. The mother hugs a teddy bear soaking its plush in tears. Everywhere is stone and bronze that a stranger's grief cannot stain.

The veteran – just a thin remembrance of a gallant day — glancing at me crooked hipped as he salutes somebody I'll never know. Our eyes meet. Don't intrude. Stay behind the line of graveyard protocol. We nod to each other as we pass. Nothing more. Although I'd like to ask where he served in March of '44.

The grass is frozen with Advent snow. A ragged pilgrim limps his religious relics from a rusted pickup to a shining shrine. A splinter from the True Cross. Bless me save me forgive me. A bloody thread from the Shroud. Mary and Joseph are picnicking on the road to Bethlehem today. The Christian year dies. Promises are recalled. We suffer our regret.

I bet you know all the Montmartre whackos living here.

All I've brought today are two suitcase photographs. The first is George Nakash's '44 portrait of you. *The Golden Girl.* Honey coloured skin and hair. Blue eyed innocence. The Westmount debutante.

I have wrapped the photograph in clear plastic to protect it and I'm standing it on a small easel by your Memorial. Perhaps the limping pilgrim will like my little shrine. If he notices. He is lost amongst his own relics.

I think about '44. The Advent days of World War II. March is the Great Escape. June is D-Day.

The Golden Girl. Alice's thick blonde hair and honey tinted skin tones brought her to the attention of Montreal photographer George Nakash in 1944. He hung this Golden Girl portrait prominently in his studio. The McCord Museum displayed the portrait in its concourse during the 1981 Nakash Exhibit.

Photo courtesy of the McCord Museum. MP-1981.133.1.85

The year begins. Ted Trafford junior engineer Shell Oil runs four shallow well drill strings at Lago Grande, Venezuela, while thinking of a skiing holiday in Canada. He books three weeks with his mother in the Laurentians. The Alpine Inn.

You are in George Nakash's Montreal studio. Hold it there he says from behind the camera.

Number 13 is in the tunnel. Jens Müller. He pauses to say goodbye to his handiwork. The bellows that pump oxygen.

A Friday evening of dancing at the Alpine Inn.

The shutter of George Nakash's camera clicks.

The beginning of your end begins. Jens is free. Nakash hangs his '44 portrait of the Golden Girl in his gallery.

You are at the top in 1944. Healthy and only 20 years old. McGill. The world is your oyster. John writes, "Dear Alice, The Golden Girl picture is still displayed at Nakash's. Right in the best place too. Holy smokes what did you do to the man to make him do that? All my love."

The Allied troops take the beach at Normandy. The war is almost over.

You stagger 37 years later broken heeled to the McCord Museum exhibition in Montreal. Half your bra empty. The Golden Girl is featured in the glass case by the entrance. You bring me back a copy of the book *Nakash*, inscribed: "To Tyler—with dearest love from 'The Golden Girl.'" "The photo caption reads: "Alice Tyler of Westmount. The print was originally finished in sepia, a process which included a lot of gold chloride, guaranteed to last forever, but a tone which accentuated honey-coloured skin and hair."

Guaranteed to last forever!

The pilgrim chants the Apostles' Creed. "I believe…"

I hear the cadence and am standing in boarding school chapel. An inconsequential boy singing a full heart of rivers and summer stars that nobody cares to hear. My class robustly marches their Advent hymn to glory. Heralding a saviour's birth. I am impressed by superstition. I know nothing of life everlasting. I am 13 and can only understand the nothingness of cold water mornings, horse sweat, Dead Man's Flats, and Mum.

What odd moments you string together.

Here is my second photograph. You'll see the connection. Fifteen years ago I climb the hall stairs and ask are you awake? I have a new horse. Here's a picture. Caressing it softly with fingertips, as if dream connecting the swirls of flanks and foreheads, you whisper, "When you ride, think of the Golden Girl sometimes."

You sleep and do not hear me say the horse's name is Emily, after Emily Dickinson. I read to you:

To fight aloud, is very brave—
But gallanter, I know
Who charge within the bosom
The Cavalry of Woe—

Like you, Emily punctuates the Woe with dashes. Far more gallant you than me I cavalry charge.

What's comforting about your cemetery is the absence of normality. Nobody talks and everybody listens.

THE MARACAIBO HOSPITAL

We would ride without talking until lunch. Then me eating a sandwich you laughing more stories. They weren't about us, but they were. The truth is always about us, nobody else.

Tell all the Truth but tell it slant—

Our poet Emily Dickinson said.
In the navy blue suitcase I carry your life after The Jens Album. He, too, had a suitcase. Big X worried that it might not fit through the tunnel. As if Jens who knew the narrow height and width as well as anybody would make a mistake. What did he pack? Probably only what a Norwegian electrician would take when working away from home. Leaving behind photographs books letters.

At Eden Brook I read aloud the small slants of while married to Ted stories—telegrams, excerpts of letters received, excerpts of letters shown me by your friends.

Tonight I write, finding order beneath your dishabille. Right or wrong it is all interpretation. Certainly Ted would tell the silly things differently.

To myself, I write a medical report about your deterioration by disease—including alcoholism as a disease not a weakness of character even though nobody knew back then—as if you were a clipboard of doctor's notes.

Alice's athleticism and drive first deserted her during the Jens gone months when she pushed herself to pass her Matriculation examinations and be accepted at McGill where, she believed, she would become a writer. The physical exhaustion of long nights. The mental exhaustion of refusing to give in to the you're wasting your time attitude of her family.

Alice's second pregnancy led to an ectopic operation in a filthy Maracaibo hospital that started her on a lifelong fight with illnesses ranging from infections to breast cancer and polymyalgia rheumatica. None of these fights were made easier by her drinking and smoking.

After the ectopic pregnancy, the specialists told her it was unlikely that she would have another child. Alone in the Maracaibo hospital, she managed a cheerful letter to Ted.

Friday June 29, 1946

My own dearest Ted,

I am so anxious to see you—I feel Wednesday will never come. There are about a million things I want to tell you. Everything seems so bloody complicated. I want to go home, or get away from here at least, and just as much, more, I want to stay here with you. Being very practical—I must go away. Since I have been here I have even had boils—they are almost gone now. But the whole thing is just a result of the bloody operation.—and Venezuela is no place to recover. However, it is impossible to discuss all this in a letter—or on the radio so we had better wait until Wednesday.

I am feeling lots and lots better. In fact my skin is even looking a fairly normal colour. I walk around quite a bit and don't sit on the bedpan any more—which is a great lift to my morale in itself.

Dorothy and Ken were all in last night. Ken is an absolute riot. Did he ever tell you the story about when he was in here—and one night some guy came along and peed in his ear! God—I thought I would roll out of bed laughing.

...Your Alice

The strain on the marriage soon followed, beginning with money problems when Bert's business slowed and he had to take a break from making investments for them. Harder to accept for Alice was Ted's loss of interest in her after the doctors told her she would not have another child. Ted, who wanted her to produce enough heirs to ensure the Trafford line would last in perpetuity, told her she was disappointing him. To wear down her ability to fight back, he began belittling any attempts she made to revive her writing.

On her way to Montreal she wrote Ted, still believing in his ability to love. Her last paragraph is all Alice style and attitude.

July 29, 1946

My dearest,

...The trip up wasn't at all bad—a little tiring. The baby was wonderful but I had to keep my mind on him and the baggage the whole time. I knit one line on my sweater—and read less than a paragraph in my book. Flying is certainly the best way to get places in a hurry. I flew up from Miami to New York—non-stop in a DC4—56 passengers. Huge thing.

...My darling—I think about you so much. I hope you are getting decent meals and not living too badly—generally. (I got the curse today so that is okay. It should be all over when I go home on Thursday or Friday.) Mummy thought I looked a little thin—but otherwise 100%—very pleased in fact.

...Well my lover—I guess that's all the news for now—oh no —H. was in the hotel at Maracaibo and his family—I snubbed them all. The bastards.

Well that's all.

Your Alice

At St. Marguerite's where she spent most of her time recovering, she soon realized she had made a mistake leaving Ted on his own. He had no intention of joining her as she recovered. He didn't need her as much as he needed money. In one letter to him she describes happiness she finds with her "bohemian" existence, hinting at the healthful simplicity in life she would seek and never find with Ted.

August 6, 1946

Dearest dearest,

John called Dad about your cable on C.W.C. shares. He has not explained it in detail to me yet, but I think he bought a thousand shares for himself and a thousand for us.

...I feel like a stinker sitting up here in all this glorious weather and you in the rotten tropics. However, my health has become an obsession with the whole family and I just wish you could see the difference already. I am dying for you to get here and get some of this air or sun or whatever it is—which makes you feel so good.

...Dad is buying the shares in his name. Tyler. OK? (We do not talk about it. He is trying to buy 2000 shares. Naturally that goes down in the books and they will know plenty about him—Does it matter as long as they are in his name? Two thousand shares is a hell of a lot and may boost the market price.)

...I am living such a bohemian existence—I have forgotten everything but you. God I love you darling—and if I had searched the whole world over I would never have found another like you. I hope you feel the same way.... It is certainly a most glowing feeling inside me—like a light that never goes out.

Your Alice

"I hope you feel the same way." I find it difficult to believe My Goodbye Mother wrote that forlorn plea.

Thirty years later, broke and in despair, Alice would write a friend:

Save a nest egg for your old age. Your children will be busy with their careers and need all they can earn. You must be able to count on yourself no matter what happens—old age, ill health whatever—at least you can be independently comfortable. I would never have believed that this could happen to me of all people. Why didn't I at least take out an insurance policy. My Dad was always giving me money for my own use. Ted's career, children's education, sports, home and so on all came first. They were so important in those days but a little common sense would have helped.

From Venezuela, Shell transferred Ted to Egypt where the marriage almost ended when he began an affair. Alice left him and returned to Montreal again. There, Big Marjorie unsympathetically insisted Alice forgive her husband and return to Egypt after he had written the first of many letters she would receive over the next 55 years with the common apologetic theme: "I promise I'll never be that way again — if you'd only come back."

My own darling,

I just knew right away when your telegram came that there was something wrong; I guess because you didn't put "all well" on it like you usually do.

Gosh darling, how I miss you. I rushed back from Hurghada Wed. morning — then no Alice on the plane. Then your telegram saying "probably" Sat. and now it looks like it won't be till next week some time. This sort of life is no good. Can't sleep, no appetite, and all on edge. I stretch out my hand in bed and nothing there —

I love you so and when you are away I think about how mean I sometimes am and then I promise I'll <u>never</u> be that way again — if you'd only come back. And I wonder how I could even get mad at little Teddy and right now I could forgive him even if he wet his pants, covered the house in paint, tore up the furniture and broke all the crockery.

Well, time for a beer, a pink gin, and lunch then to lie down and dream of you and love, and then wake up and realise I am alone.

All my love my angel — my sweetheart and kisses to Teddy.

Your Ted
XXX

His promise, of course, was never kept. How strange for me to recall Jens's promise to return for his Alice, and the risk he took to keep it.

But Alice took Ted at his word and returned to Egypt where, three years after the doctors had told her she would not have a second child, I was born.

For 13 years she would unpredictably hug me and laugh as she whispered in my hair, "You are my miracle. Nobody expected you after Maracaibo. You are my miracle."

She was mine.

ALL BETS ARE OFF

Big Marjorie died in 1948, age 48. Alice didn't attend the funeral.

In the early 1950s, we moved from Egypt to Calgary, following Bert's astute business advice to get in on the ground floor of the oil business there—Imperial Oil had made its Leduc Number 1 discovery in 1947 bringing oilmen from around the world to make their fortunes in Alberta.

When Bert unexpectedly died in 1954, age 53, Alice and Ted rushed to Montreal to collect their inheritance. There was nothing! It had all been spent on the family's show-off lifestyle. A shock more than a surprise to find expectations wrongly counted on.

According to Ted's calculations, all bets were off! The Tylers had not lived up to their end of the marriage bargain and now he wasn't obliged to live up to his end. He was free to do as he pleased. Which he did.

With the little money Alice received from her father's estate she bought a farm in Springbank overlooking the Rocky Mountains west of Calgary, and built a house.

I was ten and my father sensed that I had him figured out. He went from mostly ignoring me to harassing me, smacking me when I was daydreaming, taking away what he called privileges—no more reading books all afternoon. There are tasks waiting outside for you. He knew my weak spot—my mother. Somehow my mother falling down the stairs was my fault, my black eye. For the rest of my life, all he had to do to stick a knife in me was shake his head sorrowfully and say, "You're going to kill your mother if you keep that up." I heard that a lot.

At Springbank, with Ted enjoying his privileges elsewhere, Alice's drinking began sliding from the fun and exciting stage to the problem stage. To her credit she recognized what was happening, as she wrote a friend:

I have been through one crisis after another and all because of damned alcohol. At last I have the problem licked but must continue to work at a program. It may sound grim to you but I am happier, healthier and wiser than ever before. You should see me ski now. — Fantastic. And I am never tired or bored any more. Ted is not too pleased as I am extremely active. It is the only way that I can find peace. Hopeless when I fuss around the house day after day.

Despite her best intentions, she could never quit drinking or smoking. Later, the scarring to her lungs from breast cancer radiation (age 53) would diminish their already tobacco damaged capacity so much that she would become reliant on supplementary oxygen whenever she was tired or stressed — both of which increased in frequency as Ted found new ways to humiliate her. For the last few years of her life she lived with her "friend" — an oxygen machine who pulsed constantly by her bed. She had another friend to accompany her — a portable machine — when she left the house. As much as she tried to laugh this dependency off, it would twist my heart to see the once strong Alice stumbling from the doorstep to the street.

Worse for her was her almost paralyzing lack of energy — the soul destroying symptom of polymyalgia rheumatica. Her fast jumping mind would battle physical fatigue every day, leading to frustration and more drinking. The only exercise she could handle some days was pouring a drink.

For Ted, Alice's progressing illnesses and drinking were the perfect excuses to seek solace for his burdens in the arms of other, more sympathetic women.

THE HANGMAN'S NOOSE

Too hard to bring this letter written by you to a friend. I read it an evening alone at the Eden Brook gate and drive home.

Dear _____

I am so sorry if I sounded upset on the phone this morning. It
just seems Ted has piled so much on me & you called when I felt I
couldn't bear another problem. You called when I really needed you.
I must find a way—really a place—where I can escape from him for
periods of time. Really this man can upset people so badly and enjoys
doing it. Now he is very happy with himself.

These days I feel I have been given a second life [after a breast
implant] and not even Ted is going to spoil that. I guess the girl in
Paris made a hell of a scene. Her name is R_____. She flew over to
London—Can you imagine?! Ted had given her _____'s phone and
address and even he was involved. It is so degrading to all of us. I am
so disappointed in _____ but I don't think he had much choice. Ted
just dragged him into the whole mess. You can't help wondering if
he has just come home to restore himself for the next one. I have lost
faith and trust and respect for him.

We sit forward on the downstairs couch. You are unleaning back very calm.
You know what I think about Ted. You know I don't want to talk about it

202

anymore. But there we are, side by side, and you say you have something to show me.

A white cut-out cardboard figure the size of a playing card dangling from a hangman's noose. The limbs connected by threads. When you hold it up to show me the limbs jerk just like the last breath spasm legs and arms of horse thieves strung up by vigilantes.

One of Dad's girlfriends sent you this.

You put it away and then tell me Dad is being blackmailed with photographs. Rather than pay the blackmail this time he has shown you the photographs.

You say you have the divorce papers this time but can't go through with it. You pay as you always have and not just with money. You won't break up the family.

And in the fading light at Eden Brook's gate, I still marvel at the love it took to break me out.

PREDNISONE AND VODKA

It has been a month since I last brought this suitcase overflowing with you to Eden Brook. I see from your father's letter it took you a much longer time to die than your mother who dragged it out for 13 years:

> There is not much more for me to say — I love you all and it will
> take a long time for me to get over this shock although it is not really
> a shock as I have been living under this sword for exactly 13 years.
> Don't worry about me — I will be alright.

You hung on for over 40 years, and every year celebrated what might be — you never know — your last birthday. Towards the end you didn't leave your room except for parties requiring an entrance. A handful of Prednisone, a shot of vodka, two shots of vodka, three shots of vodka, and we'll put "my goddamn friend" in the car. "I'll be the life of the party." Or the corpse. A drunk on steroids.

P and V you call it. You look full of Piss and Vinegar you would say as I rode from the cabin. P and V.

Now it's Prednisone and Vodka.

Between your perennial Might Be Last Birthdays and Last Christmases on Earth I'd stop by to say hello.

I open the front door quietly, hoping you are sleeping. Climb the carpeted stair, say hello to Thomas Samuel Trafford, Dad's moustached 17th century progenitor hanging like a guilty conscience above the stairs. His noble legacy reduced to this. I stop momentarily to smile at the repair in the canvas where you slashed it with the ceremonial sword that authenticates the Trafford family legend of once being held in high esteem by people who mattered. Important people. Royal people. Good for you giving the pompous Thomas Samuel something factual to reconsider his descendants by. He commissioned several portraits to ensure his immortality. Over the years I noticed somebody had switched one intact inheritance for the one you slashed. Maybe it never happened. Like the women that never happened. That thought finished by the top of the stairs. Truce. Stop. Look and listen. Like a careful child crossing a street. Not the way you raced me across Eighth Avenue to the Bay. Not the little girl Alice you told me about who got lost in downtown Montreal and was taken to the police station and given ice cream. No, that child said when her mother came. She's not my mother. Is there more ice cream? We watched the grizzlies behind the cabin tearing up our garbage. Nothing to worry about you told me. Aren't they gorgeous? Craziness.

You make more sense to me asleep so I go slow down the hall to your room, hoping you are in bed, curled on your right side. Your painful left arm on a pillow. A *New Yorker* folded beside you. The TV on.

You are the lone survivor of a high speed cancer alcohol and polymyalgia rollover. Casual paramedics say to me we've done this before. Poke tubes in your nose filtering oxygen into your radiation and nicotine burned lungs. Your left breast sliced off by the windshield. I'm the boy standing by the roadside. Left behind as they rush you to the Holy Cross. Your fight flickering down like the fading siren.

They cut away everything better to be safe jagged steering wheel operation tearing out the lymph glands so your arm is permanently swollen like a fat person's jellied thigh bulging below tight underwear. Better than dying too soon. Polymyalgia jams you into passive tired low gear. An insurance write-off. Prolong life. Throw a handful of steroids in the vodka and your cylinders fire cursing anger. Revived but your drunk driving brain wiring too tangled for repairs. No turn signals. No brake lights. Short circuits. Accusations. You're awake now. Where are you going? Who are you so mad at?

Staggering from your bed to your bathroom to your recliner. Dragging your plastic oxygen tubes. Living on hidden chocolate and vodka. Your belly sagging more each day.

I sit on the straight back chair and you wave me closer. They have stolen everything from me the vodka says.

What does it matter Mum? Be like Santiago and fight the sharks the best you can. They cannot steal love. Nobody can steal love. Only trinkets. Scarves. Rings. We had 13 years of good weather Mum. We know love is always on the platform waiting for the train to leave. We find it at the Mount Assiniboine horse camp. It lives in the Dolly Varden we caught in the Bow River. Nobody can steal a truly big fish. Even if it is only a small boy's small fish. Nobody can steal love.

Live with forgiveness now. Let them steal it all. Make it a gift. No thank you expected.

XXX OOO
Tyler

PARADE DAY

You are always in my best childhood days. Like the blue sunshine sprinkling through summer poplar leaves. I lay back on the Eden Brook lawn, hands beneath my head, and the warm splash of you soothes all my too lates away.

When Dad's oilman's office was in the Wales Hotel I leaned as far out the windows as I dared and waved my cowboy hat and shouted Up Here as the Stampede Parade passed below. Every year I'd go down to the fairgrounds and you'd lead me through the barns to where chuckwagon drivers tapped hard fingers on tobacco cans and tucked a pinch of black chew under their lips. Looking at you under their hat brims. Beautiful. Strong too, I would send back to them their horses dozing in the sunlit dust of the barns and alleys.

We'd wander the rabbits and chickens and ducks and jams and pies and vegetables and bundles of wheat. We'd watch the farm kids milk the cows and drive teams of black tail swaying Percherons not scared at all. Whoa they called leaning back on the wagon seat to stop the team at the door. They kicked the brake down and jumped off while dads helped them unhitch.

Behind the chutes the rodeo cowboys warmed up their roping horses swinging loops back and forth cantering circles. Blue jeans spurs leather boots straw hats smokes hanging from their lips. Bronc riders and bull riders sitting on their heels along the fence. I wanted to be a cowboy with a lariat and hear the announcer on the loudspeaker as I backed my horse into the chute: Tyler Trafford from Calgary Alberta on Gold Dust.

Gold Dust was my Springbank horse. A blonde chestnut with a silver mane and tail. I had plans for us. She argued about everything.

At night the Stampede fireworks would boom over the fairgrounds and when we got home I wouldn't even try to sleep this dream. I couldn't stop thinking about all I could be.

Then I was eleven and a lot bigger. Almost grown up and you let me be my not sleeping dream for a morning. There was an accent voiced horse trainer you knew. Rolf. Where did you meet these Montmartre cowboys? That summer he said he would ride in the parade. He didn't have anything parade fancy. A yellow slicker. Hat. Boots. He was just going for the ride. No ribbons. And you said I could go ride too even though Dad had tasks lined up for me.

Rolf came early that morning in his fender dented pickup and we jumped Gold Dust in beside his black. Everybody was asleep but you. I remember you waving goodbye from the driveway and saying you would watch for us in the parade. I leaned out the truck window and waved back as we turned the corner.

Rolf drove us to the end of Ninth Avenue and unloaded the horses. He helped me on and said go find some kids your own age to ride with. When the parade's over meet me back here. I rode up Ninth Avenue until I met some other kids riding horses and as soon as there was a break in the floats we trotted in and joined the parade.

We whooped and hollered all the way, waving our hats to everybody. And we got lots of cheers. The other kids had more cowboy stuff. Slickers and saddle bags and vests with pearl snaps and string ties. I just had the stuff I always wore but Gold Dust looked real good all brushed and eyes wide open when the fire crews blew their sirens.

Afterwards I rode through the streets to find the truck and wait for Rolf. He shows up an hour later and almost falls off his horse. He slurs about meeting some other cowboys and I could tell they'd had a wild Stampede time. Me too.

As soon as I got home I asked if you'd seen me in the parade and did you get a picture of me. No you said. Things came up and Dad decided not to go.

I felt genuine cowboy even if I didn't have a yellow slicker tied on my saddle. You listened for more than an hour while I talked about me and my exciting life.

I was too young to know I should thank you for giving this life to me. Then, but not now.

THE INHERITANCE TABLE

Fighting back begins with a Cambridge Grace. *Benedictus benedicat.* May the Blessed One give a blessing.

You goddamned cheating English bastard you shout throwing the silver pepper shaker. It misses Dad, skims the glass doors of the china cabinet and breaks against the wall.

The silver pepper shaker is part of his inheritance and engraved with a family crest. Your arm is still good. You missed intentionally.

The battle zone is a long mahogany table inlaid with thoughts like I hate you and you made another great throw between the heavy Corinthian candlesticks. In the night I see the kitchen lights of Springbank farm families passing the mashed potatoes and gravy.

Eight of us sit at Dad's inheritance table on Sunday evenings for Family Dinner. You make roast beef, roast potatoes, peas, creamed onions, and salad. Dad carves the roast in the kitchen while we stand in line until he is ready to assign the slices. No greediness. Go wash your hands. Then we sit down and wait. You and Dad at the ends, three children on one side, three on the other. Teddy away. We can't pick up our knives and forks until Dad picks up his.

Sit up straight. Knife in your right hand, fork in your left. Don't talk with your mouth full. If it's not offered don't ask for it. Line your knife and fork up in the centre of your plate when you are done. Don't ask for seconds. Wait to be asked.

Dad's family ring on his little finger taps the table. His only sign of nervousness. Don't make a scene he says.

You goddamned cheating English bastard. Is this what they teach at Cambridge?

Silence. Just the tapping of a family ring on a mahogany table. A table where nobody remembers anything. Nobody says they are sorry. This is the scripture of the family table.

You lean back in your chair. Her name dances on the table. The others eat with eyes nowhere to look. Dad eats as slow as ever. Always the last one finished. He meets my eyes. "You're an aggravating son of a bitch." I don't look away.

Nobody wants a second helping. Who dares? Later we will creep down the back stairs for a peanut butter sandwich. Now we wait. Knives and forks lined up in the centre of our plates. He stands, his chair scraping on the blood red tile floor.

That's right run off you say.

Whose task is it to do the dishes? he asks ignoring you.

The corporate hierarchy is posted in the kitchen. Name ordered by age. Task. Time to Complete. Clear the table. Rinse the dishes. Load the dishwasher. Empty the dishwasher. Clean the counters. Clean the table. Set out the breakfast dishes. You need to learn responsibility. Your mother needs your help now. We can't hire help when your mother is like this. It is her fault. Now set an example. Time to be a man. I'm eleven years old.

In the night Geoff and Billy make sandwiches and chocolate milk. I go down the dark stairs to the long cupboard in the basement where more of Dad's ancestral proof is stored. It smells of damp newspaper. Inlaid wood chests from Natal. Leather boxes locked. Shotguns, riding boots, cigarette cases, Bibles, chocolate boxes of letters, hand mirrors. This silver framed photograph is his parents. Edward and Sya. Edward like Dad and like Teddy. We're not allowed in here. I remember when this inheritance arrived at the train station. I remember the carpenter building this long shelved cupboard. Upstairs the men delivered new old dressers and chairs and the dining-room table. Everything is Dad's and now he's not like everybody else. He's not ordinary. Look at the engraving on this tray. Superior. Appraised. Important. Valuable. Insured. Mum's got no inheritance. None of this is hers. No family table. No ring that taps between the silences. No heavy leather book of proper English family history.

You are asleep on the couch and I can't wake you.

I want to tell you I don't care about any inheritances, not if they make the room smell of damp newspaper and make Dad a cheating English bastard. Family crest. Family ring. Family Dinner. Family table inlaid with thoughts like I hate you.

It always ends with a Cambridge Grace. *Benedicto benedicatur.* Let praise be given to the Blessed One.

THE WRITING DESK

I am watching you at your elegant, glass front desk, writing letters non-stop, page after page. I am sitting quietly and watching, memorizing your intensity. Wishing now I could fit your desk into Alice's Suitcase.

I see the bookcase top with a double curve over two glass doors where you lined up your hardcover editions of Browning, Defoe, Carlyle, Tennyson, and a collection of anthologies, notably the English Romantics (William Blake, our visionary!)

Below the books are cubbyholes and slots where you kept letters, photographs, paper, and envelopes. Then the fold down writing surface supported by smooth sliding braces. Opening and closing with a gentle click. Then the four lower drawers. Maybe, but unlikely, you kept The Jens Album in one of them.

Years after I received The Campbell's Soup Box, Dad relinquished this desk, giving it to me according to your request. I can't write on it. Maybe one day. In the meantime, it encourages me. Write who you are. Nothing else matters. "It's a fuck of a life if you don't live your own way. It's a fuck of a story if you don't tell it your own way."

I am baptized. Never forget the smell of alone. Never forget who you are today. Never let go of who you are.

Hidden inside the desk behind cubbyhole drawers — places no surreptitious searcher guessed — I find your treasures of pressed memory flowers and photographs. Hidden in the leaves of your books are private notes, more photographs, and more pressed flowers. Your stowaway companions. Everyone fooled by the always open desk where, I like to think, you planned my post baptism confirmation class of living like Alice.

Here's a long hidden Note To Self* slipped smoothly from a narrow tunnel not detected. It makes me remember My Goodbye Mother.

Tyler has bought a huge yellow school bus which he is converting to a home on wheels. I think he plans to write poetry and books and just take the world as he finds it. Very idealistic and drives Ted crazy. I adore him and envy him.

Inside the glass cabinet of the desk I keep the silver cup that Grandfather Bert sent to Egypt shortly after I was born.

July 20, 1949

My dear Alice—

I am so happy about your baby and cannot wait to hear all the details. We are sending you a silver cup (engraved) for him.
    Love Love,

                        Dad

Alongside the cup I keep what Ted thought was your ashtray. I didn't tell him what it was—a postcard size, silver tray so tarnished that I had to polish it gently to read the faint inscription mirror written: *Albert and Marjorie Tyler are pleased to announce the engagement of their daughter Alice Patricia.* The printing plate for your engagement cards.

Ted has promised to give me the Duncan Crockford painting of our cabin at Canmore that you told him I should have. We'll see. If I get it, I'll hang it near the desk. Addendum to Alice's Suitcase.

A GUN ROOM STYLE

Here I am with the washed ashore debris of your Ted belittled writing. Him the master of Cambridge essays. You the fast no going back wonder changer of life into words.

I see pregnant mothers today reading books or playing music for their unborn babies in the hopes that the baby will develop better than regular kids. My Goodbye Mother didn't know anything about that, or the dangers of smoking and drinking while pregnant. But when she was told she couldn't have more children, she resumed her writing with the same determination she had at McGill. Despite Big Marjorie's disparagement. Despite Ted's eloquent criticism. She kept at her stories until I was born. Then she quit and began to teach me how to care, how to laugh, and how to live my own life. I became her possibilities.

I began to read when I was four, a little trick we kept to ourselves until I started school. And, like her, the *New Yorker* was my favourite. Maybe that's why I read and my brother Geoff loves the avalanching heartbeat of testing danger...a Goodbye Mother attitude people admired, envied, or loathed.

Alice's writing must have been under way when she was in her early teens. Slipped beside *Robinson Crusoe* I found a thin book of poetry written by Kenneth O. Macleod. I don't know his relationship to Alice other than he is the Montreal author of a non-fiction book about Birks (as in the engagement ring Bert bought). He inscribed his work with "Again to dear Alice, 'Memories of Summer 1941.' Ken."

I found one package of encouraging letters written to her by Wilf (married to sister Marjorie) after word spread that Alice would not have a second child. On the first letter, she wrote: "* NB: Wallet to read daily," and "* Show Tyler." I do not recall her showing the letter to me, but if I did see it, I probably would not have understood the hope it gave her—that she could have a life not entirely run by Ted…or, I suppose, Big Marjorie…or maybe I wasn't paying attention.

November 11, 1946

Hello Dear Alice—the Blonde Bombshell—

Keep up the writing kid, first to me and second to work on the great Venezuelan novel. Stick to it chum, although I will admit that it is an awful bloody chore. The novel, not me. I tried to.

…But you Alice will continue to write—no giving up. Presently, doggedly, with the head drooping and spirit battered to shreds.…It is in you dear and it will come out.

…Now I'll tell you what you're gonna do. Forget the novel for the time being. Too long. Too difficult for a start. Decide that you are going to write for the S.E. Post, or Colliers, or etc. Study the Post, if that is the one, to note the type of story, the length and the illustrations. Lay off any continued story because that is the most difficult kind and anyway that would bring you back into novel length. Grind out a typical magazine story (reading time 15 minutes) (30 minutes if you are a lip mover) and arrange with Ewing Krainin, 538 Fifth Avenue to hand it around N.Y. for you. He knows the people who decide what gets printed. If you can do the above in six months you'll set a new record for speed. Honest. However it can be done only if you write each day. That's what the successful writers of today do. If you try to write every second day you are beaten. That's what they say. Even a half-hour per day will do the trick but it must be every day.

…Love from CWB

Wilf, the only one in Alice's family to encourage her writing, sent other letters admiring her gun room style and sense of humour.

January 9, 1947

Hello Dear Alice,

Thank you for your nice letter; your style is very good although your language may be described as invigorating. Very refreshing, not unlike a strong breeze from the gun room.

Are we to have a second Hemingway? Answer me that, kid.

How is the writing, chum? Time to start pitching again? Lower your sights dear and stop aiming your writing at the New Yorker. They seem to demand a sophisticated writing in their stories that only an experienced craftsman can turn out. Also, they pay nothing and that means $100, at most. St. Eve. Post will accept a simpler type of writing, will pay $1000 and eventually when you are fat and famous, $5000. Of course, then, you can write for the N.Y. for the fun of it. Study the Post. How about a story of the old Venezuelan aristocracy and what became of them?

…Love to Ted, Teddy and yuh.

Instead of Venezuelan aristocracy, Alice writes back a dissertation on "sanitary units." I wonder if even Wilf appreciated the irony of this substitution for aristocracy. It took me a moment to catch.

February 22, 1947

Hello Dear Alice—

I love your last letter. It's wonderful. I don't think I have ever read one more funny. It appeals especially to my type of sense of humour. It is certainly a thoughtful dissertation on the progress of civilisation as evidenced by the availability of sanitary units. You have everything except the illustrations.

…All the best

CWB

FOREVER YOUNG

This is the only excerpt of a story written by Alice that I found. I have no idea of its date, and that adds to its importance to me.

The months passed—years passed. More and more men and women —fell—never to return. The Europeans kept coming. The Norwegians were such heroes to us. They skied and jumped off our mountains in a marvellous style we had never seen before.

One Norwegian Jens Müller came often from "Little Norway." We grew fond of each other and when the day came for him to leave he promised to return for me. Too soon I heard he had been shot down.

Those who die and those who we can no longer see live on in our hearts. There are times when anticipation is better than realisation. Jens lives on in my heart. He is forever young.

THE LAST LETTER YOU WROTE ME

Just before she died, Alice asked me to do a quiet something for her. It doesn't matter now what it was. A few days later I received my last letter from her:

My dearest Tyler—

Every day I thank the Lord for letting me share in the life of a very special human being.

I thank you so much for what you have done—your sacrifice has not gone unnoticed.

Your action has wisdom and integrity seldom seen in society today.

Thank you Tyler for your great gift. It has lifted my spirits—God knows I need that before I leave for eternity.

Love you forever.

Mum XX

THEY NEVER CAME BACK

I am in a claustrophobic tunnel. The what if crumbling walls of a tunnel leading to a railway platform are fast burying me.

It took one year for the tunnel named Harry to be completed. One moonless night earlier and Jens's telegram would have reached you before your engagement to Ted. I cannot think about you and Jens anymore.

I midnight wake and wander to Eden Brook. I have to write about the you I carry.

I was twelve years old in Mr. Redekop's grade eight class at the Springbank School. You didn't know Mr. Redekop. My last teacher you met was Mrs. Bilton at Elbow Park School, grade three, when you talked her into letting me be in her class even though I didn't know handwriting. I was on my own in school after that.

My best friend at Springbank was Ron Anderson who had a white-faced horse named Baldy and his own room in the basement of his house where nobody touched his stuff. He had to work hard at home doing farm chores. He could lift a bale of hay onto a pickup. When he was allowed we would ride in the bush and pastures by the Elbow River. I think we were close to Eden Brook except it was a cow pasture then. Ron and I knew the gates and how to stretch the wire fences down to cross without gates. We had sandwiches smashed up in plastic bread bags and a fort. We lived dangerous lives.

When I wasn't riding with Ron or by myself or looking after my rabbits and pigeons, I was building a cross country course for my horse Gold Dust. I let the rabbits play on the lawn when it was quiet. I was waiting for the right day to let my homing pigeons take their first flight. I planned to tie an important message on their legs that would surprise me later.

You brought home barrels and rails for my cross country course. Mostly I piled up brush and logs. You borrowed an orange City of Calgary street barricade. My course went through the trees and made loops. Some jumps you had to go over a couple of times from different directions. There was a slide down a pile of loam and another over a bank and onto an abandoned road. The best part was the final sprint up a laneway towards home with bush on both sides. That's where I put the barricade and two barrels because I needed a lot of speed to get Gold Dust over the big ones. You would wait for me to race up the laneway. I didn't have a stopwatch but I had an official finish line. You held panting Gold Dust like you were our groom waiting for the results. We were champions.

You let me do anything. One other place I liked to jump but didn't tell you about was on the Atkins' land. (Can you believe they rented that land from Mrs. Bilton's family?) Anyway, I found four rocks about a horse length wide on the side of the hill. Two were small for warm-ups. Two were high enough to be scary. They looked like cement filled with rough rocks. I looked rocks up in the *Encyclopaedia Britannica* in the boys' room and figured out conglomerates. It took a lot of speed to get Gold Dust over them. The truth is she didn't like jumping. She didn't like anything much except oats. I had to head Gold Dust home fast and then veer her over the rocks. She was more likely to try if she thought it would get her back to the oats sooner.

You didn't ask a lot of questions. Neither did I.

For a couple of years on Saturdays Teddy and I and sometimes Geoff would ride down the Banff Coach Road and over the Trans-Canada Highway to Milli Pratt's for Pony Club. That took all day. That's where I saw teenagers jumping over proper jumps and practising for horse shows. I went to some shows with Gold Dust but to have a chance of winning you had to have a better horse. You and I talked about that. We found one named Ebenezer. A chestnut with four white socks. And he could jump at least four feet and junior classes had smaller jumps than that and I knew Ebenezer was for me. Milli Pratt agreed. He was going to cost $2,000. We had to talk to Dad.

No.

That was the last time he made me cry. Age twelve.

He had his own plans for me I was to find out later.

That summer he told me I had to write some tests, to see how I was doing in school. It was a kind of game. He made it sound like fun. He would time me. It sounded like a race. I did my best to do well. I finished early. Later I found out how stupid I was. While he was marking the tests I rode Gold Dust as fast as I could over my cross-country course.

When I got back he told me I had been careless. He knew that I could have done better if I hadn't hurried so much. But it was important to be honest so he had sent in the scores.

For my birthday in July you had a party for me and my friends from school and most of them brought their brothers and sisters. I have the picture you took of them all standing around my 13 birthday cake candles. Just a bunch of regular kids, except the boys who hayed and had big farm muscles.

A few weeks later Dad said the results had come back from my tests and I had done very well and had been accepted except there was a final interview. That's when I was told I would be going to boarding school in the fall. You didn't say anything.

I went alone to the interview at a hotel and met the headmaster. Mr. Ned Larsen who had hair just like Dad brushed back black and Vitalis shiny. He pointed out I was 13 which was young for grade nine but they were willing to see how I did. I was going to get a bursary which was something I had never heard of. I had more important questions to ask.

Was there going to be riding? Could we have horses? Well, you can't have your own horse but you can go riding. A couple of boys go riding and I could go with them. And what about skiing? Oh yes. There was skiing. Bring your skis after Christmas.

The interview ended and I was thinking about it. I wasn't sure if I was going to say yes. I waited for you and Dad to ask if I had made up my mind. The only thing you said to me was I had to go with you to buy boarding school clothes. The school had sent a list and we had to get everything on it. Oh. I'm going.

I decided it was time to try out the pigeons. I opened the door and they flew out circling higher and higher into the sky until they disappeared. All

I could do was stand there watching and wondering what had gone wrong. They never came back.

I met a couple of older boys on the CPR platform in Calgary saying goodbye to their parents. Dad was shaking hands with the other men proud of their sons heading off to be trained as the leaders of tomorrow. Not telling them what an aggravating son of a bitch his son had turned out to be. And glad to see him go.

You stood by yourself. Just watching. You never said anything. That's when we began to have a lot of before then things not to talk about. I wasted four years there and felt sorry for myself a lot. Now I feel more sorry for you.

The school was on Vancouver Island. I had no idea how far it was from the train tracks at Old Canmore. It took all night to get to Vancouver where a bus took us to the ferry and then to the school. I was 13 and would never live at home again. I phoned collect Sunday nights to say hello. Not long until I would become the Christmas and summer holidays visitor growing up and away from five brothers and a sister with family stories I'll never be in.

I'll never forget waking up that first morning in a dormitory with ten strangers. I didn't know where I was. Everybody laughed when I asked about the horses and the skiing. This was a British school. This was Shawnigan Lake School. SLS. Your name is Trafford. Just like your father's at Cambridge. You will be playing rugby and cricket and there are house prefects and school prefects and school ties and house ties and blazers with crests and chapel every morning and study time after dinner and bells that ring when it is time for class and bells that ring when it is time to sit down to eat and ring when it is time to stand up and bath schedules and lists posted of exam results and do anything wrong you get defaulters working for an hour in the garden supervised by prefects and shine those shoes and fix your collar and stand up when the master comes in the class and say good morning sir.

Aren't we smart in grade nine learning Latin except for Trafford a lazy boy who will fail in life and never be a prefect or a leader of tomorrow. All but Mr. Dickens who taught English and said he would prefer if his class stayed in their seats and kept reading.

My only regret was that I didn't keep the letters you wrote me. Almost every week I got your rolling circle writing the way you talked that should have been in the *New Yorker* and nobody knew but me. You made me laugh so

I could know you loved me but there's other interesting things to write about too. Mr. Ross, the publisher of the *New Yorker*, you wrote, said everything could be explained or described by a writer. Even on blue crinkly paper I love you can't stay hidden long in scenes and personalities. You wrote the way you think. Who else could write wonderful like that with no going back edits? And probably drunk. Hemingway. Henry Miller. Old friends of yours.

In Mr. Dickens's class we memorized poetry and analyzed essays and compared and contrasted, similes say things are like other things, and wrote model paragraphs so we would be prepared for our matriculation exams. Mr. Dickens signed J.E.D. taught me the mechanics. Forgive my misplaced modifiers and alliteration trespassing but I cared more for the voice writing letters signed:

XXX OOO
Love Mum

Sometimes I would write for J.E.D. the way you were teaching me and he would note Interesting. On the school term's one creative writing class topic of What You Did This Summer, I wrote in no going back style an essay that I titled How To Teach English. It came back without a comment. The mark on the top left in black: 55%. I looked across the aisle to see the mark on the nailbiter's: 88%. It was about what he did that summer. I asked J.E.D. about the why of this. His three words of mystery described my destiny as a writer.

Go sit down.

I came home that Christmas and things were okay until I said something wrong and you started drinking and Dad said what did I come home for — to cause this trouble? All the money spent on school and these are your marks? It is time for you to be a man. Say sorry to your mother. You're upsetting her. Don't ruin this Christmas for her.

At the dinner table I face surrounding disapproval of my siblings. He controls them now. But not me. I am the outcast. Not in this story anymore.

One June morning the headmaster asked me after chapel if I would like to stay back a year to be in a class with boys more my own age. I wasn't doing well he said. He was Ned the two-faced Nickle with Ted's untrustworthy hair. I had this figured out already. I asked why would I stay in school an extra year.

The back of his headmaster gown whirled his answer down the chapel hill. The next semester I had a desk in the dumb class. The only time he talked to me after that was when he caned me six for being even dumber and not trying in my studies. He had just announced that university entrance requirements were going up and from now we at SLS would set 60 percent as our standard. Public school 50 percent wouldn't be acceptable for leaders of tomorrow. Bend over for six more checking my full of sloth underpants for extra layers.

I was 16 when I graduated. The bus took me out the gates and I never went back. It was lucky for Canada I wasn't a leader of tomorrow. I knew how to conjugate love in Latin. *Amo. Amas. Amat.* I love. He loves. You love. But I had forgotten what love was.

Dad said the family was moving to Australia and my mother wasn't well and it would be best for everybody if I stayed in Calgary that fall and continued my studies.

I turned 17 that summer and I saw you the next summer in Sydney and you were passed out on your bed. I didn't know you. Dad said I had made things worse. Again. I'll always be an aggravating son of a bitch and he can tell I'm going to turn out just like her.

HE JUST LAUGHS

Undated

People always seem to want to take things. . . . My biggest mistake was giving my money to Ted . . . Men use money as power. Power at work, power socially and most awful power over women — particularly their wives. I don't want Ted's meanness to rub off on me. When two people live together they grow alike.

If I could just cope with keeping our home running and a part time job, it would be great. When Ted — no, when I allow Ted to upset me I am very disorganized. That is the real answer. Just don't react to his ever changing moods. He just laughs when he sees how much he can disturb me. For him it is all a joke because I cannot, no one can, hurt him. He has learned or taught himself that he can do no wrong and he is very content with that belief.

ST. VALENTINE'S DAY

On your birthday your Memorial Inscription still looks wrong to me.

TRAFFORD

EDWARD LE M   ALICE TYLER

1917 –   1924 – 2004

I have a copy of the form you signed as purchaser of Plot 1920 Space A, with a Wheat Bronze Memorial, and Latin Cross Emblem and Inscription. There was no mistaking your rolling signature. Whether I liked it or not, this is what you wanted.

I have kept that form on my desk for two years. I glance at it every day wondering why it looks wrong to me. I study it with an Emily *"tell all the truth but tell it slant."*

After I went to Montreal and Uncle John showed me your mother's grave, I understood why you chose to use your maiden name, Alice Tyler, for the Memorial Inscription. Because that is the way your mother's inscription reads: Marjorie Flanagan Tyler 1901-1948. Her maiden name was Flanagan and her married name Tyler.

But today I looked at the Eden Brook form closely and for the first time I noticed the date you signed it: February 14, 1997. St. Valentine's Day.

What a buried message!

You never did anything thoughtlessly. You always had a reason. You intentionally chose St. Valentine's Day to select a burial plot and Memorial Inscription for you and Dad.

I know, too, that you wanted to make sure I got this no going back bronze message. You didn't leave it to me in a note or a letter that might have been lost or overlooked. This is the no anaesthetic treatment you gave Geoff holding his hand tight against the table while Dr. Anderson stitched his thumb. This message is in the unflinching set of your jaw. Take the pain. *Charge the Cavalry of Woe.*

Dad's eyesight is going. He's almost deaf. His hands shake. He's forgetful. I expect he won't last much longer. And I'm not looking forward to that. Because the day his ashes are buried beside yours will be the hardest day of my life.

But I will accept this plot and this inscription because I accept there isn't anything too painful or anybody too wrong that I can't survive with love in my heart. Because I am learning there is much of you in me. With love, we endure.

YOUR FUNERAL

Alice:

This is how I felt the day of your funeral.

I wonder how you felt the day Big Marjorie died. You never said.
XXX OOO

Tyler

DESTINATIONS

MY HAZEL-EYED INHERITANCE

I have explored the Alice Suitcase hundreds of times. In the reading now, wondering and remembering, I can fit the slants that tell one new truth: an answer to a question I'd had about myself. It begins in the June 1941, letter Jens wrote Alice as he left Canada to join the aircrews in England: "I wonder if you have ever spoken to her about our plans for the future?"

That was when I first recognized how far apart Big Marjorie and Alice lived. The mistrust must have been terrible.

Why wouldn't a daughter tell her mother about her engagement? Because Alice didn't have a mother. She had Big Marjorie.

And in her heart, Alice recognized that Jens was showing her a new possibility, a different role for herself—a life she chose. And she knew Big Marjorie would stop at nothing to destroy her relationship with Jens because it threatened her own ambitions. Big Marjorie had a plan and Alice knew she wasn't going to be allowed to ruin it.

Alice seldom spoke to me about her family. When she did, she always said how much she loved her father, Bert, and how handsome and athletic her brother John was. She mentioned half-sister Marjorie rarely, and always with sadness. She tried to say good things about competing sister Joan. But her mother didn't get a word. Big Marjorie lived behind the door Alice never opened. Marjorie Tyler 1901-1948. My grandmother. The never mentioned.

For Alice, who understood irony best of all, the greatest irony was that Big Marjorie did not leave her children the promised perfect happiness of horse shows, debutante parties, and Westmount mansions. She only left them her unhappiness.

What would Big Marjorie have thought of Emily's ambition—

If I can stop one Heart from breaking,
I shall not live in vain

Big Marjorie lived in vain and in vanity.

I never doubted My Goodbye Mother loved me, but there were days when she didn't want me to visit. Her jaw would be set hard and her hold me close blue eyes would become a slammed shut door. I called them her loveless days. They had nothing to do with P and V. They were coherent. Even as a boy I knew there was a never ask me hidden behind her eyes slammed shut.

It wasn't until I opened The Campbell's Soup Box that I knew it wasn't a what, it was a who. Big Marjorie.

As I began to understand the relationship between Alice and Big Marjorie, I could feel my teeth clenching and my stomach tightening. The anxiety I felt wasn't for Alice. It was for me. Because I was seeing in Big Marjorie a piece of myself I had never admitted before.

I inherited Big Marjorie's hazel eyes and dark hair. I inherited her small hands. And I inherited her traits. I know they are genetic because nobody taught me how to be envious, vengeful, greedy, hateful, and selfish. I am a natural.

I know this because every unhappiness in my life has begun in moments when it seemed easy to be envious, vengeful, greedy, hateful, or selfish. This was the Big Marjorie side of Alice a small boy never saw. She kept that door locked to protect me. For my thirteen young years her arms surrounded me and all I knew was a nothingness that loved me and I loved in return.

My Goodbye Mother kept the door locked on Big Marjorie as long as she could. Silver labelled Smirnoff Vodka the key to that lock. One drink alone to insert the key. One fall down the stairs to turn it. One more drink that never stops and unhappiness is your life.

And so My Goodbye Mother takes me to the train station.

I couldn't know then how painful it was for her to send me away, to ease my life the aching. I was only thinking about myself.

Now that I recognize the love wrapped in her goodbye, it is too late to thank her. What I had interpreted as rejection was actually the most wonderful gesture a mother could make. She had baptized me and it had taken. I was strong enough to survive on my own.

Today, years away, I continually discover, often horrifically, that I can survive but not defeat my inheritance from Big Marjorie. It is with me forever. I can only control it.

In my worst times, I recall cold eyes warning me: Don't let this happen to you.

For My Goodbye Mother, I write the following so my children will know how hard she fought her inheritance. I write in her voice because I am all the voice she has left.

Debu-Tramps and Dunderheads

My name is Alice Tyler and I grew up in Westmount, a wealthy city inside Montreal, during the 1930s. The Depression, as other people called it, did not involve my family any more than the War that followed involved us. Depression and War were polite dinner discussions about inconveniences we would never experience...Until I met and lost my Jens.

It's all gone now. That's what I should be writing.

My crowd absolutely adored each other. We spoke English, attended Anglican or Catholic churches, and our mothers approved who we would marry. We went to the same schools, attended the same coming out parties, and holidayed together in the Laurentians. We were upper class — sophisticated. We were politely nice to servants — shopkeepers — gardeners. We could afford to be politely nice when it suited us.

None of that matters. If it ever did, it shouldn't have. But here it is anyway. Written like some goddamn English term paper. Boring.

We lived on Lansdowne Avenue, which climbs through Westmount and intersects at the top with Westmount Boulevard. Our house had only seven bedrooms — As my father was reminded at least once a week. I had my own bedroom, which didn't keep my sisters from snooping through my desk and closet. My parents didn't sleep together — It wasn't hard to figure out what else they didn't do together. Our cook and housekeeper Annie O'Reilly slept downstairs. Father said she was a godsend. She came to us from Ireland, 16, poor, and uneducated. She didn't like me and threatened to leave because of me. I didn't like her. My mother liked Annie because she reported everything

I did. We had an Irish Setter named Alpy. My mother—born an immigrant Flanagan in New York State—liked anything Irish. You couldn't hide your poor Irish background with a name like Flanagan, so she paraded it.

Behind her back, my mother was known as Big Marjorie. She wasn't physically big. She was quite small, with dark hair and hazel eyes filled with suspicion, and not much love. She was a user of people—manipulative, ruthless, and determined. That's what made her big. A big what?—You can guess for yourself.

The only thing she cared about was a red brick and stone mansion on top of the hill: 3803 Westmount Boulevard. She wanted to be more than admired. She wanted to be envied the way she envied other people. How tragic to love that poison.

Pathetic. I'm writing a diary of regrets. What kind of writer am I? Sitting here with a handful of steroids, a pack of cigarettes, and my Smirnoff. Who the hell do I think I am? Nobody wants to hear how I suffer anguish. The only writers worth reading live their stories in their guts and tell them without self-pity.

When my mother first came to Montreal from Malone, New York, she was snubbed by society, particularly by my father's family who thought he should have done better than marry an American who already had a child—my half-sister Marjorie.

Marjorie of Malone was not a woman who took a snubbing well. She specialized in revenge, and the revenge she planned was to move into 3803 Westmount Boulevard.

Once established in that mansion, she told us, she would be high enough in Montreal to "piss down on everybody else."

As her daughter I was part of her plan. That was my purpose in life.

I'll tell you what's gone. The Alice Tyler who had ideas. Smart ones. The girl who could write. Not this biography stuff. The laugh and see inside a story. That's what I could do. Pissed away.

Where has all my good writing gone? The last thing I wrote worth reading was when I was 25. Where has the good stuff gone?

In one way I can't blame Big Marjorie for seeing love as ending badly—it's bad enough getting dumped by one mother, and she was dumped by two.

Her father—Joe Flanagan—owned the Flanagan Hotel in Malone, where vacationing New Yorkers enjoyed the rural air in the stylish comfort of formal dining rooms and verandas. Eva, Joe's first wife, was broad-shouldered, dark-haired, and probably a more voluptuous woman than elegant Joe could handle.

Joe and Eva had two daughters. When my mother was nine—I can only guess at her age—Eva ran off to start a new life for herself in Montreal, leaving Joe and the girls behind.

Joe then married Ada who, although mean-spirited and thin, was a real millionaire. Not nouveau—like some people we would later avoid. Ada told Joe to get rid of his girls, so he dropped them off in a nearby convent.

As soon as my mother was old enough to leave the convent she got married, apparently taking the first offer to come her way—I never learned his name. He turned out to be a no-good drunk who headed for Florida never to return. Poor Marjorie—dumped again! There was no record of a divorce. However, there was a consequence—"Little" Marjorie—born in 1921.

There it is again. Me writing like vodka eroded every original thought. The steroids make me want to fight this but the only way to fight is to write and I can't. This isn't writing. This is facts worked into sentences. Writing is seeing the good and true in life and working that into sentences. Anybody—even Ted—can write grammatical facts. Next thing I know I'll be adding a timeline and family tree.

Long before she arrived in Montreal, my mother had made up her mind she was going to be looking down on the high society Flanagan Hotel guests who had ordered her to bring their summer drinks onto the veranda—All she had to do was marry the right man.

The right man was up and coming Bert Tyler who she met drinking in a Montreal speakeasy. Big Marjorie could see Bert had possibilities—He just needed a plan.

You make the money, Marjorie told him, I've got the plan. It won't be long before we'll be drinking at the Ritz-Carlton.

Bert and a college friend owned Standard Cottons, buying the ends of rolls from textile mills and reselling the fabric to retailers as remnants—A good business.

Rumours about Little Marjorie's long gone father circulated in the gossipy circles of Westmount, but Big Marjorie was adept at covering her past. One gossip claimed she was never married, and another was sure she was never divorced. My brother John says we are all illegitimate. He thinks that's a riot! But wouldn't that rip a page out of the Trafford genealogy!—A family of asterisks. Illegitimates. Bastards. Edward III*

That's some dishabille punctuation. Wouldn't get a matric with it but who cares now. It makes sense to me. Besides I'm just trying to get all this down with the least confusion as if any of it would make sense to anybody but a goddamn lunatic which is what we all were.

It makes me laugh to recall our lives. Geoffrey, always my smart aleck boy, has a tell it right saying about family facts and history—Do you want to know the truth, or do you want to be happy? After that two snorts from the bottle digression I continue—

Expecting to be well received in Montreal after she married Bert was one of the few mistakes Big Marjorie would make, as far as her own life went. She made plenty of mistakes for other people.

Whenever Ada visited us—Grandfather Joe never did—she arrived in her chauffeur driven Rolls Royce, gave us Grandfather Joe's gifts, made critical comments about my mother's taste in clothes and furnishings, and left. Only death could erase Ada from Big Marjorie's Not To Be Forgiven list. Big Marjorie kept track of everybody, and everybody was on one of her lists. When Ada died and never left my mother a dime, my mother added Ada's name to her Live Forever In Hell list. As if God wanted to help my mother get her revenge.

That was better writing. I don't get a paragraph like that too often. Tells a lot without footnotes.

Big Marjorie's plan for success began with raising her daughters as society debutantes and marrying them into the right families. Then we'd all move to the top of the ladder.

We attended Miss Edgar's and Miss Cramp's finishing school. (Lots of laughs over that name!) We were educated to smile and act as if nothing in our lives was more important than balls, dinners, and coming out parties. While the rest of Canada counted pennies during the Depression, we bought gowns.

John called us Debu-Tramps. He was right about that. Many of the girls were dunderheads—spectacularly stupid. Golf. Tennis. Dying to buy a horse and join the Mink and Manure set. Cocktail party opinions. Children. Those were our destinations. Why can't I write that wasted life into this?

We had money because, just before the war started, Bert signed an exclusive sales contract with Celanese Canada—the biggest textile mill in the area and one of the first to manufacture synthetic fabrics. Retail fabrics were hard to get, and we controlled the supply. The money rolled in.

Overnight, we went from well-off to wealthy, but not from Unacceptable to Acceptable. Despite her deserved affluence, Big Marjorie waited to buy 3803 Westmount Boulevard. First, her daughters had to be married well. Then she'd buy the house. Then the guests would be invited and they wouldn't dare make excuses. They would have to come. Then there would be gloating. Then she would be happy.

Big Marjorie ran a matrimonial outlet for me in her Lansdowne Avenue drawing room—interviewing applicants and accepting their gifts of flowers and chocolates. It was hard to say who the men were courting most ardently—my mother or me.

I have a character like Big Marjorie—a real life self-centred bitch—and I'm writing her like she's a matron with a quirky side. A godsend I'm punctuating with contrived generics. But I'm not going back. Imagine living like this and thinking you're special.

On Friday nights she drank in the speakeasies and had front row seats at the professional wrestling. She, like Eva, was a woman of contradictions, except Eva's contradictions were now starting to embarrass Big Marjorie. Eva had moved by then to the Mohawk Reserve—she'd rather live destitute with Indians than with her own daughter.

After that we were never allowed to see Eva. Whenever I asked why, my parents repeated the family story—my grandmother had abandoned her children—the most wicked sin possible—and should not be forgiven. Maybe that's one of the reasons I stuck with Ted. I know I heard it often enough.

Not content with just refusing to allow Eva to see us, Big Marjorie used us for revenge by taking us to visit Grandfather Flanagan in Malone where we always impressed everybody by throwing money around. Joe's spinster sister, Mary Flanagan, loved me especially—When she died, she left me the $1,000 that I would use to buy the land at Canmore.

Big Marjorie bought us clothes so fast that some packages were never opened after they were delivered. As if spending were her wartime duty, she directed other forces north where she and Bert bought the Alpine Inn, our year-round resort hotel two hours from Montreal. The Tylers soon had the best horses and their own stable to keep them in. And a private riding ring. And tennis courts. And a swimming pool. And a golf course. And a ski hill. And an artificial lake. Who wouldn't want to marry beautiful Alice Tyler and get his hands on that life?

I can laugh about it now, our extravagant living, but it was all a show. Out of sight my parents argued in high emotion swearing brawls. For all the horses, tennis lessons, and skiing we had, my sisters and I were taught only envy for each other — We couldn't stand to see each other succeed. Love meant being better than the other, getting more attention. My mother encouraged that love, our fighting for her approval. She was fighting her way to be the envy of Westmount society — and she raised us to struggle for the same worthless cause all our lives.

I never learned to recognize The One Good Thing when it came my way.

I know Big Marjorie believed she was well on her way to becoming a social success while I was engaged to Don. She always said she wanted the best for me, and Don was from one of the best families. He would later do very well in business, so she didn't make a mistake about him, just me. I know how disappointed she was when I gave Don back his ring. — All right, threw it back!

I don't know how much Big Marjorie guessed about me and Jens or how many of his letters she opened. She was probably pleased to know he was safely locked up in a POW camp.

Aren't I something? Big love with Jens and that's the best I can write about it. Where did that love go? Where did everything go? I should be writing about that.

The happiest I ever saw my mother was the day I told her I would marry Ted. I wasn't blind. I could see her pushing us together as soon as Ted and his mother arrived at the Alpine Inn. I could see the two mothers cooking things up. But I admit Ted was easy to fall for — handsome as hell. And I needed somebody to love. Somebody close by, not locked in a Stalag. I hardly heard from Jens even though I wrote him all the time. How could I have known about his plan to escape? Looking back, I suspect my mother intercepted more of his folded POW letters than I knew about. He always addressed them to me at Lansdowne Avenue. When I was at St. Marguerite's, my mother was supposed to forward them to me, so I know she had the opportunity to read them. She routinely blamed the War for anything that went wrong — including letters that went missing.

Jens Returns to Canada. After "The Great Escape," Jens was back in Montreal for Alice, as he had promised. This photo of Jens, Alice (centre), and Joan was the last one she saved for The Jens Album.

I can't blame Big Marjorie for the mess I found myself in with Ted—It was my own damn fault. I should have been more suspicious of how well things went with him at the Inn and how quickly our parents agreed to our engagement. It was all too easy. Imagine getting married after you've only known someone for three weeks.

I knew my mother always wanted her own way, so I should have questioned why she was so agreeable when Ted wanted us to be married in Trinidad rather than waiting until the two families could be together at the Alpine Inn and she could put on a big show. My father even bought the ring for Ted—and packed me on the train to get married. Alone. Not a Tyler at the wedding. I'm sure my sisters spread rumours that I was pregnant. My mother wasn't taking any chances. I was getting married.

Maybe that was the day I lost writing true. All that not facing up to my heart. If you don't live it you can't write it. Biography is all I have left. There was so little of me in my life that I can barely remember it happening. Who the hell was I? Or more to the point who the hell did I think I was?

When I look back on those spring days in 1944, I see my mother was worried for good reason about motorcycle racing war hero Jens. If she'd been reading his letters, she'd have known we were in love and intended on getting married when he returned for me. I remember him showing up right after my parents announced my engagement to Ted. What a coincidence! There he was. As calm and loving me as much as ever — on his motorcycle outside our house — as if escaping from a Nazi POW camp were nothing compared to keeping his promise to me. I'll never forget that ride on his motorcycle. The way he drove so fast took my breath away. He was a slow lover. That took my breath away too. My mother really grilled me after that. She must have been worried that I'd escape too.

I could have built that getting grilled scene more truthfully. Everybody was lying and the scene avoids it. No truth. No good. And I'm avoiding writing anything about sex. What happened to that?

Jens met me at the train station to say goodbye the day my father and I went to New York. It was a sad parting for both of us. We knew how we felt. We'd talked it over enough since he'd come back for me that we didn't have anything left to say but goodbye. He would always be a beautiful person to me. The most honest person I would ever know. He deserved better than me. And it wasn't until that movie came out that I knew what he had done to keep his promise. My Jens.

My father didn't grill me the way Big Marjorie did but I could tell from his face that he was wondering whether I would make it to Trinidad after he left me in New York. He was wondering if I'd head back to Jens. — I wasn't going to. I'd chosen my destination. I didn't have a clue how wrong a marriage could go. Maybe it wouldn't have worked out with Jens, but I would have had a hell of a lot better chance.

There should be a bullet fired in every paragraph. Minimum. I'm writing like a self-absorbed Whiner! If I ever say I should have would have then I know I didn't believe in myself enough. That's the sign. It was there and I just let it go. You always know what's right — and what's the easy way out. The wrong ticket. The wrong destination.

I didn't see Big Marjorie until I came back to Montreal with Teddy, my first child. I was recovering from an operation and was a mess—I had boils and I was exhausted. My mother fussed over Teddy more than she had ever fussed over me. She liked to call him Edward III—as if he were royalty and she were a dowager princess.

Ted and I were already having money problems. If it hadn't been for my father making investments for us, we could never have lived the way we did in Venezuela. Ted's salary as a junior engineer wasn't as great as everyone guessed, and he never saved. Whenever the unexpected came up, we were broke. I had to cash one of my father's investments to pay my fare to Montreal. Otherwise Ted would have left me to recover or die in that dirty Maracaibo hospital while he stayed in the drilling field.

Big Marjorie was sick in bed when I got to Montreal. The doctors could never discover what was wrong with her. I had almost recovered—I even played a little tennis on our courts by the lake—but I had to wait on her hand and foot like everybody else. She said she had made a big sacrifice for me coming all the way up to St. Marguerite's so I could be with my friends. She only got out of bed in the afternoons and we had to bring Teddy, blankets, and tea onto the porch for her. Nobody said anything, but her complaining was driving everyone around the bend. My father stayed in Montreal. I don't blame him.

Even today—when I'm stuck in a sickbed—I think about the way Big Marjorie rang her silver bell and bossed everybody around from her bedroom. I catch myself being just like her sometimes. She blamed her unhappiness on sacrificing everything she could have had so her thankless children and husband could have a better life than hers.—I blame mine on Prednisone and Vodka. Nobody believes their unhappiness is their own fault—or that they can't do anything about it.

Why is it so hard to write twisted reality? Your problems are ok. But if you want people to care about what you are writing... what did you do about your problems? Go to Paris? Don't be a loser. Feel what's right then do it. Use your own words. Why did I plot a second-hand life for myself?

Bert bought 3803 Westmount Boulevard for Marjorie after the war. It was rundown and he had to put over $100,000 into repairs before she would move in. Imagine how much money that was—I bought our first house in Calgary for $6,000 with my stock market profits.—I got a good tip on a

Redwater well. The Westmount mansion had two bedrooms on the third floor, each with double windows opening over the neighbourhood below. My mother slept in one bedroom, my father in the other. She liked standing in the window and looking down the hill at the people below. — I bet she lifted her skirt a couple of times just to see how it felt.

That's descriptive. There's an image to keep readers awake at night.

Bert told me life with Big Marjorie on Westmount Boulevard was terrible. He had expected the new house would make her happy, but it didn't. My sisters, always looking for the dirt, suspected he was carrying on with Hazel, my mother's nurse.

Big Marjorie was on oxygen the last month of her life, like I have been for years. She died in January 1948, age 48. I didn't go to the funeral. The church was full so I probably wasn't missed. Joanie wrote me about the carloads of flowers and said it was the biggest and most beautiful funeral that year in Montreal. That would have made Big Marjorie happy. She died at the top of Westmount Boulevard and had a grand funeral. An accomplishment.

I find the ending to her life to be a sad unaccomplishment. I try to think well of her. She was no dunderhead — she should have used her brains for something better than manipulating people to get what she wanted. Big Marjorie believed getting what you want was a desirable quality in a mother. She taught it to me and I had to learn the hard way that only love can fill the emptiness in your heart.

I loved my mother — but I didn't like her. It is hard to like someone who values public displays of wealth and social status more than she values her family. When I think about the Westmount mansion, the horse shows at the Alpine Inn, our debutante balls, coming out parties, engagement parties, wedding parties, and even her expensive funeral, I think of them as excuses for her not asking me what I really wanted — to be a writer. I feel like Big Marjorie was always saying to me — "You must feel loved. Just look at all I am sacrificing for you. Look at how other people envy you. What else is there in life?"

I didn't feel loved, at least not by her.

More whining. Not interesting.

I let myself believe that Ted was offering me what I wanted. And Jens, in

Big Marjorie's Ambition. Owning this hilltop Westmount mansion became an obsession for Alice's mother, and she would spend the last years of her life there gloating over those who had snubbed her during her less glamorous days.

Stalag Luft III, had no prospects. I must have been crazy not to see what he was really offering me.

Getting back to the twisted version of love my mother learned from Joe, Eva, Ada, and convent life. She interpreted compliance as love. Maybe that's why she and Ted got along so well. They played the game with the same rules. She assumed her goals were the best for everyone, that what she wanted should be the top of everyone's agenda. In the end, all she did was spread misery.

I can see myself doing the same, especially after a few drinks. I'm like a child sometimes the way I crave attention. There's nothing I like better than commanding a room. I can't resist. It makes me feel young again. It reminds me of when I was courted and desirable. I know it drives my children up the wall, but I need the flattery that being blonde and beautiful brings me. Or used to bring me. When I think about how easily I gave up McGill and my writing, it is no wonder I looked to everybody like just another rich blonde debutante marrying a family ring. Jens saw me differently—but—well, there's no going back. I made my choice and I'll stick it through to the end.

That's better. A little truth about my life. Not a bullet but with potential to be a killer.

After my mother's funeral, the family disintegrated. Nobody knew what to do for themselves after being told what to do by her for so long. My father became depressed, drank a lot, lost interest in his business, and married my mother's nurse, Hazel, giving proof to my sisters' gossiping.

All of the beautiful Tyler children became alcoholics. I succeeded in dealing with my alcoholism—a couple of times. John would be the only one who could keep the bottle locked up. I outlived my sisters. I expect John will outlive me.

My father dropped dead in 1954, age 53. The doctors said it was a heart attack, which surprised the family because he'd just had a check-up. Everybody suspected nurse Hazel knew how to use her hypodermics to her best advantage, but that couldn't be proved. By the time she let the family into the house, she'd taken everything of value, even the gold strips my father hid for us above the door jambs.

Ted and I had moved to Calgary in 1951, on my father's advice, to get in on the oil industry just starting there. Ted joined Home Oil but planned to branch out on his own with an advance on my inheritance.

As soon as we heard my father had died, we took the first train to Montreal and began making plans for living big in Calgary. The estate lawyers told us there was nothing left for us—no millions—a few thousand for me. Everything had been spent on my parents' big lies life. Ted and I couldn't believe it. We wanted to start an investigation. Accountants. Lawyers. Detectives. All our plans were ruined. As was our marriage.

More whining.

As soon as Ted knew I wouldn't be getting the fortune he'd been expecting, he didn't waste any time getting involved with every available woman—that hurt, considering I grew up being the girl every man wanted. It rattled me, and he took advantage of my insecurity to pressure me into giving him most of the money I had kept back from my investments. As if that would convince him to keep his pants on.

No bullet but at least a laugh in that paragraph.

The land I had bought at Canmore worked out well, so I bought a farm at Springbank, west of Calgary. By then the last of my seven children had arrived, Katie and Tom. Right away, Ted had his business friends take me aside and convince me the farm was a poor venture. By the time they were finished, I had sold most of it to them...and they all made good money reselling it later. I paid to build our new house and then Ted told me I was beginning to imagine things. He kept that up until he had to tell me the blackmailers wouldn't accept imaginary money.

Even better. That laugh has some sting to it—Maybe there's still some good writing in me. Or at least enough vodka left to write the conclusion. It is going to be a close finish, but bet on the vodka. It always wins.

That was when I agreed to send Tyler to boarding school. Ted might have destroyed both of us if I hadn't. Tyler would never back down from him, and I knew I couldn't protect him much longer. Imagine not being able to protect your son from your husband.

The rest is Prednisone and Vodka haze and doesn't matter much now anyway. At least Tyler got away. Like those damn pigeons of his.

This is what I knew in my heart all along. *It's a fuck of a life if you don't write it your own way.*

MY SEARCH
FOR JENS MÜLLER

"A YOUNG WOMAN IN CANADA"

I am now living in the aftermath of The Jens Album. It caught me not paying attention and tripped me. Instead of falling into Eden Brook grass, I fall into myself. I fall into the maybe never happened memories of my forgetting place.

In the Album I found Jens who knew my laughing teasing adventurous Goodbye Mother. Jens's letters were proof that she existed. I hadn't imagined her, that I hadn't made her up inside the despair of her alcoholism, unfaithful husband, cancer, and polymyalgia.

In the Album I found Jens who loved My Goodbye Mother with all his heart. He didn't love her because she was beautiful. He didn't love her because she came from the wealthy Tyler family. He just loved her.

As I read his letters I couldn't help but think how straightforward he always was about their future. He kept reminding her that he was a fighter pilot. That he had left university to become a fighter pilot. He told her he would come back for her with nothing to offer but his love. He kept his word. Jens never considered not keeping his promise. I will come back for you.

As I read and reread the Album, I had to stop every few hours and sort through the tumbling images of Alice escaping from my heart. I didn't sleep in those first days of remembering.

When my thinking cleared, I began my search for Jens Müller:

The sun has just come up. I make coffee and turn on my computer. I try a Google search for Jens Müller. Nothing relevant. I try Jens Müller Stalag Luft III. A screen of hits.

I click on NOVA. The banner reads: GREAT ESCAPE.

Two clicks and halfway down the page is a photo of Norwegian Jens Müller. The same Jens Müller who is in the Album.

The same Jens Müller!

The endless falling into myself. You are not in your urn at Eden Brook. You are here in my hands in this Album. This is you. For sixty years you kept yourself hidden. I sit by the window wondering if you will just happen to drive by.

I quit. Stop. No more. It is weeks before I can resume my search for Jens Müller. He must be famous. It will be easy to find him. But Jens Müller, it turned out, did not want to be found too easily. Jens Müller would always be poker-faced.

In my email inquiries to embassies and war museums, I said I had photographs of Jens Müller taken during his training in Canada. I never mentioned the Alice/Jens romance. I thought it best to keep it private until I could discuss it with Jens. I decided that, if nothing else, Jens deserved to know that Alice had kept all his letters and photographs.

I hoped he would want to meet me.

With each email I included a little silent piece of my love for Alice, hoping it would help my inquiries find the right destination — Jens.

It would be months before I picked up his trail. Nobody but me, it seemed, was interested in what happened to Jens after the war. On May 10, 2005, I received a helpful response from a director of the Norwegian Air Force Museum. He told me about Cato Guhnfeldt, a journalist in Oslo who had written several books on Norwegian fighter pilots.

In early May 2005, I sent Cato an email asking if he could help me contact Jens's family and if he knew of any sources for more information on Jens.

By coincidence, I had just found an email address for Jon Müller, Jens's son, on a Great Escape website and I sent this message:

Hello

My name is Tyler Trafford and I live in Calgary, Alberta, Canada. I have some photos of your father taken in Canada where he was training as a fighter pilot.

I would like to send you copies if you are interested.

Tyler Trafford

On May 11, I received replies from Cato Guhnfeldt and from Jon Müller.

And My Goodbye Mother's blue eyes laugh as she figures out where I found Jens's Messages From The Grave.

Hello Tyler

I would be delighted. I have just one photo of my father in front of a 331 sqd spitfire. I have managed to make a PDF copy of my father's book on the "great escape" but it is a 20Mb file so it's hard to send it as attachment but I could put a stamp on it. Interested?

Regards / Jon Müller

I almost fell off my chair when I read the second paragraph of Cato's email.

Did you know that he had a Canadian girlfriend that went to school in Montreal? Müller flew a Hurricane in 1941 that carried the school emblem of his girlfriend. I have a photo of Müller and a girl at a Canadian ski resort. Maybe it was the resort your mother's family ran?

It was nice to hear from you. Look forward to hear from you again.

Best regards
Cato Guhnfeldt

One question answered. Jens had died five or six years ago.

I still wasn't prepared to reveal to anyone that I had Jens's love letters to Alice, so I continued my email correspondence with Cato and Jon on the basis of the photographs. Still, I was hoping to find out more about Jon and the rest of the Müller family. Cato subsequently sent me several emails full of information on Jens, the plane he crashed in training, and the plane he flew in his early fighter missions on which he had painted Alice's school crest.

Then came a second, even more startling email from Jon.

Hello Tyler

My father mentioned a few times that there had been a young woman in Canada but he never mentioned any names, but I know he received a Christmas card every year and I suppose this could have been from Alice.

Regards / Jon Müller

Alice mailed hundreds of Christmas cards every year, most with a personal note, so it made sense to me that Jens would receive one. I suddenly felt as if Alice was with me, smiling each year as she slipped a card for Jens into the pile of mail going to the post office.

A week later I received this information from Cato:

Dear Tyler

Further to my email to you sent earlier this evening. Jens Einar Müller was born in Shanghai in China in 1917, but grew up in Oslo. He took his first civilian pilots licence in 1935, and after finishing high school went to study in Zürich, Switzerland, to become an engineer. In 1940 he travelled with fellow Norwegian students to France and sailed with a ship from Bordeaux, first to England, then to the US, where he travelled to Toronto to train as a fighter pilot.

Müller joined the Norwegian airline company DNL in 1946. DNL soon afterwards became a founding company for SAS. Müller stayed with the airline until 1977, and retired on his 60th birthday that year. In retirement he worked on a local farm, took up carpentry, built his own villa (where Jon now lives) outside Oslo. He also worked restoring old furniture. He died in April 1999.

Jens Müller met his future wife Liv in SAS, where she worked as a flight stewardess. Together they got two sons, Jon and Einar. Liv Müller, by the way, is still alive.

Thought this would be of interest to you.

Best regards
Cato Guhnfeldt in Oslo

I sent Jon and Cato a few emails after that, just to keep in touch, but I had lost my enthusiasm for following up that part of Alice's story. Hearing that Jens had died in 1999 had taken away the possibility that I would ever have the chance to talk to the man who had loved his Dearest Alice.

I began writing My Goodbye Mother stories for her, visiting her at Eden Brook, and talking with her few friends. For 16 months that seemed to be enough.

In the fall of 2006 I began having claustrophobic nightmares in which I was trapped in metal boxes, jail cells, sinking ships, and even sewers. In the morning I'd crawl out of bed tired after a night of fighting with sheets and blankets. It should have been obvious where I was being trapped each night, but it wasn't. It took months of thinking to realize that, like Alice and Jens, I was a prisoner. Jens in Stalag Luft III. Alice in Big Marjorie's scheming. Me in the memory of the life I had had with My Goodbye Mother.

It was an unexpected realization. After 40 years of forgetting, I had unearthed My Goodbye Mother and now I was a prisoner of those years. I was unable to live in today. I was comparing everything I was doing today to the days at Canmore. To Dolly. To the *New Yorker* cartoons. I was desperate to escape.

I sent Jon Müller an email. I hoped that knowing how Jens had fared after his escape would give me courage to make my own escape.

Monday, October 30, 2006

Jon

It has been a long time since we communicated.

I have been working on some stories about my mother's life and now I think your father had a bigger influence on her than I first realized. Would you be willing to talk to me about your father if I came to Norway? I am trying to arrange a trip to Europe in February.

I would also like to meet Cato Guhnfeldt. If you would like to meet me and hear what I have learned about our parents, let me know.

I also understand that discussing events from 60 years ago isn't too interesting for everybody.

Tyler Trafford

Jon replied the next day.

Hello Tyler

Yes, that would be very interesting, meeting you, and to hear about our parents.

I have talked a little with Cato. Sadly, his father passed away a few weeks ago.

Jon

I left for Norway on February 22, 2007.

SANDVIKA, NORWAY

I still hadn't told Jon the depths of the Alice and Jens romance and why it had ended. I didn't know how I was going to do that until I had met him. He lived in Sandvika, a 45-minute train ride south of Oslo. We would meet in the train station. Train stations!

You never know how people are going to react to revelations about their parents. Here I was going to Norway to meet Jens's son, and I hadn't yet told my five brothers and one sister from another story about The Jens Album.

Perhaps, I thought as the plane left the Calgary runway and there was no going back for me, when I tell Jon about Alice he will suggest I spend the weekend in the train station.

Jon met me after a small, nervous mix-up at the Sandvika train station. As soon as I shook his hand, I knew the weekend would go well. He's tall like Jens, but with a heavier build. Soft-spoken, calm, and self-confident. He's about the same age as me.

We drove to his house where I met Grete, his wife. I was fighting to stay alert after my 18-hour flight. As we had a small meal, chicken I think, and a glass of wine by the fireplace, I wondered if I should wait until the morning to tell them what I knew about Jens and Alice.

Jon and Grete sat opposite me as I thanked them for the meal. Then Jon said, "Tell us why you are here." That was blunt. For me, it was now or never.

I told them everything I knew about Alice and Jens. About the Alpine Inn. Big Marjorie. Jens's letters from Little Norway and London. The secrecy.

McGill. The arrived too late letter sent days before his escape from Stalag Luft III. My mother's life after 1944.

Everything. I gave them my blood.

I finished by handing Jon a binder with all the photocopied letters. "Read them," I said.

He took the binder to the dining-room table and began to flip through the pages. Then I noticed him wiping a tear from the corner of his right eye. He saw me watching him read and said, "Thank you. I never knew this side of my father."

I went to bed a few minutes later and left him and Grete alone with Jens's letters.

In the morning, Saturday, we talked a little more about the letters and about Jens.

My father and I built this house, Jon told me. Mostly my father, he added. He was meticulous. After we had the foundation poured, we had a crew of carpenters come to raise the house walls. They repeatedly checked the accuracy of the foundation before telling us that the foundations were correct within a few millimetres. They'd never seen work like that before. That was my father, Jon said.

Then Jon and Grete offered to take me to see Jens's grave. I had been imagining a World War II Memorial with a Memorial Inscription commemorating Jens's escape from Stalag Luft III.

At the cemetery, Jon and Grete brushed the snow off a lichen covered boulder. This was Jens's Memorial: 6,725 kilometres (4,179 miles) from Alice's Memorial at Eden Brook.

When Jens died, Jon went to their favourite meadow and found a boulder he could carry home. Just as he and his father had preferred to do everything themselves—a familiar to me attitude—Jon neatly chiselled the Memorial Inscription into the boulder:

Jens Einar Müller. *30-11-1917 / 30-3-1999.

"My father was an atheist," Jon replied when I asked about Jens's religion.

While I heard many stories about Jens over the weekend, nothing told me more about Jens than that boulder. Jens thought of himself as an ordinary

Jens's Memorial, Norway. The unassuming boulder and inscription are the
Müller family's acknowledgment of Jens's modesty and steadiness.
Photo courtesy of Jon Müller.

man. Nobody special. He lived that way, he died that way, and was buried
by his family that way.

Jens, an ordinary man, must have been an enigma to Big Marjorie for
whom being ordinary was the same as being second class.

Jon, Grete, and I drove around Sandvika for several more hours as they
pointed out places that were significant to Jens, but all the time I thought
about that inconspicuous boulder. I hadn't been in Norway 24 hours and
already I knew why Alice had loved Jens.

He was her One Good Thing.

In the afternoon we stopped by the apartment of Jon and Grete's daughter, Mari. She is in her early 20s and lives with her boyfriend Henrik, whose birthday it was that day. Mari had a cake and coffee prepared. I sat in a quiet corner while Mari's and Henrik's families visited. Morten, Mari's brother, dropped by.

Jon and Grete's children are about the same ages as Judy's and mine. Mari is 24, Morten 27. Morten is a musician, a heavy metal guitar player, and very serious about his band. Mari is studying English and American literature history at Oslo University and wants to work in publishing.

As I listened to the families speaking Norwegian, it struck me how many coincidences there were between Jon and me. To start, our names: John (Tyler) and Jon. Our wives, Judy and Grete, both work at colleges. The colleges are "sisters" and have numerous exchange programs. We both have a boy and a girl. The boys, Nic and Morten, are musical. The girls are...different. Mari is involved in literature and publishing. Shar is in the military and has served twice in Afghanistan and will likely go back.

Jon and Grete have a cabin in the Norwegian outdoors. Judy and I have a cabin in the Canadian outdoors. Jon and I love our wives, work through life's problems with them, and would rather spend time with them than anybody else. We're friends.

In the evening the three of us talked more about Jens and Alice. I told them I sometimes wondered what would have happened if Alice and Jens had been able to marry. Jon shrugged a little, as I imagine his father would have, and thought his answer through before speaking.

"Then you and I wouldn't be here, having this evening," he said. He was right. You can't think about "what ifs."

Jon handed me a pair of hand bellows from beside the fireplace, saying his father made several like this pair when he retired, using the same leather valve that he used in the bellows that pumped fresh air into the tunnel. He pointed out where his father had burned his initials into the oak handles. JEM.

Jon stood up and said he would be back in a minute. He returned with an identical pair. "You should have these," he said, handing them to me. I wasn't sure if I should accept the gift. They were irreplaceable mementos of his father. Burned with his initials. JEM.

Jon insisted.

When I went to bed late that night, my last waking thought was that Jon was my brother. Not by birth perhaps. But in him I saw what my mother loved in Jens. She would have loved Jon as a son. I would have loved him as a brother.

The next morning Grete took photographs of Jon and me. In the one I like best we are standing under one of the timber beams that Jens designed and installed. Both of us are standing with our weight on our right foot, our left crossed over and with our thumbs in the pockets of our blue jeans. He's taller than me. But we are brothers.

Come downstairs and look at the shop where my father and I worked, he said to me after the photographs were taken. The shop was like Jens's escape: perfectly planned. The wrenches, saws, hammers…everything…all in order. Maybe it was too late for me to meet Jens, but I could see him alive in this shop.

A row of knives in leather scabbards hung on the wall. Jon handed me one. My father made these knives and did the leather work, he said. I asked if he had a sewing machine to make the scabbard. No. He did it by hand. I shook my head in disbelief. The stitches were so uniform that it was impossible to see any variance that would indicate they had been sewn by hand. Later, Jon showed me a leather motorcycle pack he had made for himself. The stitches were just as accurate.

Jon Müller and Tyler.
Jon welcomed Tyler into the Müller family home in 2007, an experience that helped Tyler understand the Jens who loved Alice.

Jon then told me about the knife his father made in Stalag Luft III. "In the camp Jens was a carpenter, and he wanted to make himself a folding knife. So he managed to get hold of a pair of skates to use for the blade.

"First he removed the skate blade from the boot and untempered it. He had some years earlier been an apprentice in a foundry and had a good knowledge of iron, steel.

"To untemper the steel he put the blade in the stove until it became dark red, took it out and let it cool down slowly.

"Then he shaped the blade and put a rough edge on it, all with a small hand file. For the hole he had a drill bit but no drill so he had to use a pair of pliers to twist the drill bit and push it down with his other hand. Took some time to make the hole.

"With this the knife blade was finished, apart from the tempering. To temper it he again put it in the stove, but this time the blade was heated until blue—try it yourself with a piece of scrap steel—then the blue steel had to be cooled down quickly. He dropped the blade into a bucket of cold water, but it went into the water at an angle. This caused the long blade to cool down at a different rate on the two sides, and the blade actually split along the middle.

"Weeks and maybe months of work down the drain!!

"So he set to work on the second steel from the ice skates and succeeded this time. The knife was put to good use and when he was ready for the escape he handed the knife over to a fellow prisoner who would remain in the camp.

"I would love to have that knife!"

After Jens retired as a commercial pilot, Jon said, he made knives for all the members of his family, and one extra. Jon handed me that knife and said:

"You should have this."

It was my turn to wipe the tears from the corner of my eye. (The knife and bellows are in the glass cabinet of Alice's writing desk, beside me as I write this.)

My emotions settled down shortly afterwards and we looked through family albums. Several photos of Jens with Morten and Mari reminded me that Jens was a grandfather as well as a hero. In the photos, there was little of the hero to be seen, and a lot of a grandfather's love for Mari and Morten.

In showing me an album of Jon and Grete's cabin and motorcycling holidays, Jon frequently stopped at photos that, to me, seemed barely noteworthy. A sandwich by the road, a rest along a hiking trail, a glass of wine on a terrace. It wasn't until we were near the end of the album that I caught on to Jon's way of thinking. They had visited some special places, including Stalag Luft III, but it was the roadside stops that he considered the most important.

"That's us," he would say as he pointed to one of these photos.

"That's us. Just enjoying life."

That phrase would become the way I would remember the Müller family. People who are just enjoying life.

That was how I remembered My Goodbye Mother. As somebody who was showing me how to enjoy my life. Riding my horse. Skiing. Reading a book. Hiking in the mountains. Being ordinary and doing ordinary things. Just enjoying life.

No wonder Jens was a refreshing, unexpected wave that swept over Alice at the Alpine Inn. The Tyler family, as Uncle John told me, were show-offs. Big, important people putting on big, important displays. Everything was big. Very big. Their friends and businesses doing very well. The path of their unhappiness.

And then she met Jens. Just a Norwegian fighter pilot. Just loving her, determined to survive the war and return to marry her. Jens. Her One Good Thing.

Maybe their life together wouldn't have worked out. Maybe she wouldn't have been content too long with just enjoying life. I'll never know.

I asked Jon about the Christmas cards Jens had received from Canada every year. He told me his father opened them without saying anything and then they disappeared. His mother Liv knew about them and would sometimes make a disparaging remark about "that woman." But his father never said who they were from. The cards are long lost, Jon explained, so we'll never know for sure. We both think about that for a moment and then change the topic.

What aren't lost are Jens's POW dogtags, he said. He showed them to me, stamped with Stalag Luft 3 and his identification, Nr. 296. His father must have worn them through the tunnel and to Britain. I expect he believed if he were caught, the tags would assure him of reasonable treatment as a recaptured POW. How wrong he was. He would have been shot in the head.

That evening Grete and Jon prepared a special meal of roast reindeer, and invited Mari, Morten, and Cato to join us. (Liv, Jon's mother, was not well enough to join us.) I was looking forward to meeting Cato. He has been a journalist at the *Aftenposten* newspaper since 1980 and has written histories of the Norwegian Air Force and the air war in Norway. Cato has an almost photographic memory and gave us detailed accounts of the war in Norway and of Jens's experiences after his escape from Stalag Luft III. Jens's modesty stood out in all the stories Cato told. Even in Jens's subsequent career as a pilot with Scandinavian Airlines he rarely mentioned his wartime experiences. The only time he acted less than ordinary was when he was responsible for training pilots. Then, he was so demanding few students were capable of passing the standard he set—perfect.

After dinner, Cato had to make a long drive home but, as he was saying goodbye to me, he told me that he had once quizzed Jens about the girlfriend in Canada, and Jens had told him it was Alice Tyler. That was a kind, unguarded confirmation by Cato, and I wished I had more time to spend with him.

Jon drove me to the train station the next morning. We said our goodbyes knowing but not saying how well the weekend had turned out for both of us. But it was there, in his eyes. Unlike his father, Jon is not poker-faced.

I couldn't sleep in the aircraft. I passed the time deciding what memories I would most like to recall of my meeting with the Müller family. The one I chose was the reindeer dinner with Jon, Grete, Mari, Morten, and Cato, and with Jens's uniform jacket hanging behind us and Alice's collection of Jens's letters on a table nearby.

My favourite story of the evening, the one that epitomizes Jens for me, was Jon's description of his father at the premiere of *The Great Escape* film in London, 1963.

As Jens and his wife, Liv, were walking toward the theatre, he noticed a large crowd gathering outside. Telling his wife the crowd must be waiting for somebody important to arrive, he found a back door into the theatre.

Inside, he asked who the crowd in front was waiting for. The answer was, "They are all waiting for Jens Müller to arrive."

Back in Calgary, I spent three days looking through my Jens/Alice pictures and letters and my photographs of Norway to make an album for the Müllers.

This was the letter that accompanied the album I sent them:

March 24, 2007

Jon, Grete, Morten and Mari:

Until I sat down to write this letter, I hadn't thought of the significance of today's date. It is also Judy's birthday, which I mention just to keep my life's priorities right.

I hope you enjoy this Jens and Alice Album as much as I enjoyed assembling it for you. The photos from Alice's Album, the ones I received from Jon and Cato, and the ones Jon and I took in Norway are filled with new and old memories for me, and all of them good.

When I arrived in Norway last month and was standing at the Sandvika train station...and no Jon...I wondered if I had made a mistake bringing this story to you. As it turned out, Jon was on the platform up the stairs waiting for me, and by the end of the weekend when I said goodbye to Jon on the same platform I knew I had not made a mistake.

Meeting you assured me that Alice had good reason to love Jens as she did. I am sure Jens would be very proud of his family today with your diverse interests and talents. At the risk of sounding sentimental, I will tell you that when I returned to Canada I told Judy that I felt very close to Jon, as if he were a brother I wished I had...except he is so much bigger than me and would probably have roughed me up a lot.

I also told Judy that I had never heard anyone describe a scene as well as Jon did when he was showing me pictures of his motorcycle and hiking journeys. "This is us," he would begin. Then he would pause before adding, "Just enjoying life."

Well, I like to think that phrase describes how my mother and Jens spent their time together. Of course, we can drive ourselves mad wondering about "what ifs" so I will not think too much about Jens and Alice's romance and its possibilities; instead, I will be happy that I took a chance and bought a plane ticket to Norway. I admit, though, that I like to wonder if Alice and Jens were watching while we ate reindeer, drank wine by the fire, looked through old letters, and told stories about our own lives.

I am enclosing an ornament from a pioneer's wood-burning cookstove that Judy and I collected while riding through an old homestead. We found this piece of "Canada" in the grass and have had it hanging on our cabin wall for years. Now it can hang on your cabin wall as a reminder of us when you are "Just enjoying life."

Tyler

After I sent my Jens and Alice Album to the Müllers, I wrote one more Goodbye Mother story.

On her birthday, October 24, 2007, I went to Eden Brook, where I read it aloud.

A BOY WITH A HORSE

I found you once lost in The Campbell's Soup Box. I found you patient in the kitchen when I planned to run away from home, age six. You packed jam sandwiches for me. You never asked anything, not where I was going or what I was going to do. You let me walk down 38th Avenue wearing my favourite red shirt and blue jeans. I had a problem and it was up to me to keep walking until I solved it.

I found you fishing on the Gulf Stream. I found in you a truly big fish that a fisherman keeps in his heart forever. I found you in Santiago written with a new ending. I found you at Old Canmore when the crippled cowboy unloaded a brown mare, a horse of my own. A life of my own. I was eight and you showed me I could go anywhere, do anything.

You knew what you were choosing when you married Ted, and you knew what you were doing when you left me The Jens Album.

In that Campbell's Soup Box you committed yourself to the life you chose. You had a fuck you answer to booze, betrayal, and cancer. You had a love you answer to every question I asked.

I find you on this afternoon of October 24, 2007, as I stand by your grave. Alice Tyler 1924-2004. I have brought one letter from The Jens Album and a pack of matches. I light the My Dearest Alice corner of the letter. It is time to cremate what is finished.

You baptized me to never let go of who I am. I will always be a boy with a horse of his own and you will always be My One Good Thing…the heart that swings me high into the saddle of nothingness.

Goodbye. My Mother.
XXX OOO
Tyler

ACKNOWLEDGEMENTS

The author would like to thank his agent, Carolyn Swayze, and her associate, Kris Rothstein, for their persistence, editors John Sweet and Paula Sarson for their commitment to this book, and Goose Lane Editions.

Every reasonable effort has been made to secure permissions where necessary. Attributed excerpts from the following appear in the text:

The Great Escape by Paul Brickhill, drawings by Ley Kenyon, copyright 1970. Published by Latimer Trend & Co Ltd.

Excerpt from "Part One: Life XVI" from *The Complete Poems of Emily Dickinson* by Emily Dickinson, edited by Thomas H. Johnson, copyright 1960. Published by Little, Brown & Company Limited.

Excerpt from "Tell All The Truth" from *The Complete Poems of Emily Dickinson* by Emily Dickinson, edited by Thomas H. Johnson, copyright 1960. Published by Little, Brown & Company Limited.

Excerpt from "Part One: Life VI" from *The Complete Poems of Emily Dickinson* by Emily Dickinson, edited by Thomas H. Johnson, copyright 1960. Published by Little, Brown & Company Limited.

Nakash by Betty Guernsey, copyright 1981. Published by Fides.

"Three Got Away" (unpublished manuscript) by Jens Müller. Reprinted by permission of Jon Müller.

TYLER TRAFFORD worked as a reporter, editor, and columnist first with the *Calgary Herald,* then with the *Australian,* and later with the Fort Lauderdale *Sun Sentinel.* When he returned to Canada, he began writing biographies, histories, and works of fiction, including *The Story of Blue Eye,* shortlisted for the 2005 Grant McEwan Author's Award. He now lives in Calgary.

2013.08.19
" a good student "
二十岁就像小得不足以
谈论人生
可是二十岁也该想之人生
我想我会很努力地
去完成我的大学.
虽然始终没有出现
那个对的人
可是我还是可以一个人
很精彩地走过这
四年半
你羡慕着别人的生活

我不知你大区
别人眼里的模样.
加油吧丫头